A PLAN
LARGER THAN
I COULD DRAW

A PLAN LARGER THAN I COULD DRAW

Stories and Perspectives from the Mind and Heart

NEVILLE CLOUTEN

SIGNS
PUBLISHING®
Established 1885

Proudly published and printed in Australia by
Signs Publishing
Warburton, Victoria.

This book was
Edited by Lauren Webb
Proofread by Nathan Brown
Cover design by Shane Winfield, based on a photograph taken by Neville Clouten
    of the interior of Thorncrown Chapel, Eureka Springs, Arkansas, by architect
    E. Fay Jones FAIA.
All photographs and illustrations are by the author, unless otherwise credited.
Typeset in Berkeley Book 12/15 pt

ISBN (print edition) 978 1 922373 82 3
ISBN (ebook edition) 978 1 922373 83 0
ISBN (audiobook edition) 978 1 922373 84 7

To Norene

CONTENTS

Preface..ix

1. The Sydney Opera House.. 1
2. Europe 23
3. Through Mexico...41
4. Australian Aboriginal Art 53
5. Africa 75
6. The Three Pillars..93
7. Andrews University...111
8. Homecoming 133

Life Synopsis..143
Thanks 147

PREFACE

In 1955, the Finnish architect Alvar Aalto wrote: "There are many situations in life in which the organisation is too brutal; it is the task of the architect to give life a gentler structure."[1]

This statement still carries truth—if not more truth—today. The corporate model influences our thinking on finances, education, politics—and everything in between. It was the belief that architecture could give life a gentler structure that turned my attention towards paying more than lip service to designing for human activities.

The eight essays in this book tell stories from my life experience as a student, an architect, an academic, an artist and a traveller. Tied together by a common theme, the stories in each essay explore issues "of the mind"—as in my academic journey into research and teaching—or "from the heart"—touching emotions in the same way that art adds to the compass of life.

The first essay, on the Sydney Opera House, does both. As I commenced studies in architecture at the University of Sydney in the 1950s, the controversy around the Opera House gave me to understand the prevalence of the view that "art for art's sake" was definitely to be avoided.

Writing on the Sydney Opera House, the American architectural critic Lewis Mumford claimed that "the vaults serve no other purpose than that of demonstrating the aesthetic audacity of the designer."[2] In general, the Australian public seemed to agree. Many had little interest in mere art being built on the shore of

Sydney Harbour. Instead, they were fascinated by the threat of out-of-control building costs and changes in political leadership. New South Wales government elections were beginning to be won and lost on practical issues surrounding the construction of the Opera House. The consensus seemed to be that the Opera House should be built on the same basis as any commercial project.

Culturally competitive debate between Sydney and Melbourne, and the question of the population's preference for beaches or opera, was carried in newspaper opinion columns.

But in the midst of the turmoil, architect Robin Boyd wrote: "By accident, unexpectedly, reluctantly, Sydney is creating one of those heart-warming non-material ornaments of society which happen throughout history once a century or so."[3] And he was from Melbourne!

My life was enriched by being in Sydney during the first decade of the Opera House construction. Its influence projected me on a course that led to Europe, to further study and an academic career. These, in turn, shaped my life in other ways.

The importance of art and the emphasis on creativity within the design process are central to several essays. In others, an academic focus on research joins with a celebration of artistic quality. This is the case in the essay on Australian Aboriginal art. My interest in the scientific principles of obtaining measurements from photographs led to the experience of visiting galleries of rock paintings. A particular example near a large gallery of paintings in an isolated location in Cape York became symbolic for me.

In another essay, I describe my philosophical understanding of the importance of the three community pillars of home, church and school through examples of high-quality architecture I have visited.

The essay on Andrews University focuses on students in the Department of Architecture and design workshops. This essay also concludes with some examples of architecture—in this case churches that I consider to be of outstanding quality. I also suggest some principles that can guide in experiencing and designing appropriate church architecture.

One of the essays introduces our Kenyan daughter, Faith. She visited us in Australia in 2020. It was while she received lessons in piano and musical theory from a close friend in Martinsville, New South Wales, that the essays in this book were written with pen in hand.

For an hour and a half on two days each week, I drove to a special place nearby in one of the valleys of the Watagan hills. There I transferred indelible memories of art, architecture and travel onto paper, later fleshed out with details from my diaries. But the memories of visiting building locations around the world provided a venue to think about more than architecture. As I took the opportunity to recluse myself amid the forest luxuries of grey eucalypts and bird symphonies, I reflected on my life's journeys.

Some experiences may read as happy coincidences. But there are times where there seems to be a better alternative—a larger plan for my life.

It is a pleasure to share these memories and reflections from my life journey with you.

---

1 Cited in Aarno Ruusuvuori (Editor), *Alvar Aalto* (Helsinki: Museum of Finnish Architecture, 1978), page 50.

2 "Architecture: The Fifth Facade," *Time*, December 10, 1965, page 86.

3 Robin Boyd, "Editorial: Introduction," *Cross-Section*, 157, November 1, 1965, page 3.

1

THE SYDNEY OPERA HOUSE

Wednesday, January 30, 1957. I had been accepted into the architecture program at the University of Sydney and on this day during my first week in the big city, the morning newspapers carried headlines that the winner of the Sydney Opera House competition had been announced.

Sir Eugene Goosens, conductor of the Sydney Symphony Orchestra, initiated the idea of a significant concert hall in 1947. The premier of New South Wales, J J Cahill, took up the charge and an international competition was held for the design of an opera house. Bennelong Point was the site chosen—remarkable in that it was a large area on the harbour close to Circular Quay. It was also remarkable as it was the location for Sydney's tram sheds.

The prize-winning design was by Danish architect, Jørn Utzon. A jury of four assessors had considered 217 entries from around the world and concluded their report: "The white sail-like forms of the shell vaults relate as naturally to the Harbour as the sails of its yachts."

I was not surprised to read that Jørn Utzon was the owner of a sailing boat back in Hellebaek, Denmark. The prospect of designing a major cultural building in a beautiful harbour setting half a world away—with year-round sailing—had taken hold of his imagination. More than this, he was a young architect interested in searching for poetic solutions to design problems.

As I entered that first year of study in architecture, I became aware that H Ingham Ashworth, dean of the Faculty of Architecture at the University of Sydney, had served as chairman of the Opera House competition jury. With him was lead juror Eero Saarinen from Cranbrook, Michigan, an architect whose roots were in Finland—a country seen as a significant leader in architectural design in the 1950s. The other assessors were Sir Leslie Martin from Cambridge, England—the designer of 1952 Festival Hall in London—and the New South Wales government architect, Cobden Parks. The jurors' report issued a unanimous decision, but it was one that had not come easily—or without embarrassment.

Dean Ashworth was responsible for organising the competition entries so that the international architects on the jury could do their work of evaluation efficiently. One of his roles was to eliminate submissions that did not comply with the competition conditions. A specific requirement in the conditions was that architects should include in their submissions a rendering of the proposed building as seen from Sydney Harbour.

Dean Ashworth dutifully sorted the entries into two groups. Those that met the competition conditions were displayed on the main level of the Sydney Town Hall. Those that did not were taken to the basement—no longer in consideration. He would not waste the time of his fellow jurors. Utzon's entry was one of those that went to the basement. There was no rendering of the building from the harbour. Yet his design was not destined to remain in the discard pile.

Exactly how Utzon's design for the Opera House came to be considered with the compliant entries was the subject of many reports and rumours after the winner of the competition was announced. Newspapers and radio hosts wanted stories to share with a public who were sceptical of the design and suspicious that it would be a white elephant. One report given credence was that during the lunch break, Eero Saarinen visited the basement, pulled Utzon's submission from the stack of rejects and carried the drawings upstairs where the other three jurors had re-assembled. To his surprised associates he announced, "Gentlemen, this is the winner!" There could be little argument with the eminent juror.

With the selection of Utzon's submission for first prize, Dean Ashworth had to circumnavigate Utzon's failure to meet all the competition eligibility requirements. He secured the expertise of one of his faculty members to render the perspective of the building from the harbour that was missing from Utzon's submission. With a group of fellow students in the architecture program, I could look through the partly open door of the faculty member's office and see an incredible rendering of Utzon's Opera House taking shape. It was this rendering that accompanied Utzon's drawings when they were later presented to the public as the winning design.

The London engineer Ove Arup joined the design team soon after the winner of the competition was announced. His skills would be needed. He later described Utzon's drawings for the competition as only sketches blown up photographically to the required size. He believed Utzon had thought a good deal about the competition, "visualising the site and scale, and arriving at his basic solution, but only in the last minute had he got down to making some drawings and he really thought it would be quite useless to send them in, and he nearly didn't."[1]

It was good that he did. Modern architecture was about to take a change in direction, and the strength of Utzon's ideas would become even more important in the following decades. In the 1950s, the foundation for functional architecture of the 1960s was being carefully laid. Form was said to follow function. It was unusual for an architect in 1957 to describe a building's design in poetic terms as Jørn Utzon did. He believed the building as a whole, with the shell vaults, had only one function—"to prepare the audience for a festival."

Critics were swift to dismiss the Sydney Opera House shell vaults—the white sail-like structures—as "art for art's sake." This was only the beginning of the criticism that would be levelled at both the design and the architect. Utzon had yet to work out how the freehand lines on the competition drawings could become structural segments of three-dimensional shell vaults, thereby making construction of the building possible. This proved to be a significant problem—requiring hundreds of hours of computer time and creative collaboration between Utzon and engineer Arup.

In fact, it was Utzon who found the answer. Arriving at London airport from Copenhagen, he announced to the waiting Arup, "I have the solution to the shells." Utzon took a wooden sphere from his briefcase, disassembled it and placed the pieces on the office table. They formed a model of the vaulted roof of the Opera House, with the geometry of the sphere keeping the same curvature for each segment of the vaults. With this defined geometry, the building could be built.

During my five-year architecture program, we were taken on various field trips to significant buildings in Sydney, and we

The Sydney Opera House, completed in 1973. Architect: Jørn Utzon.

visited the Opera House more than any other building. The first part of construction was the piling—some 700 steel-cased shafts, almost a metre (3 feet) in diameter—which would support a platform as a visually strong base. The superstructure would later spring from this base. Spectators would sit on the platform, beneath the shell vaults, and participate in the completed work of art. Beneath the platform, every preparation for the opera production would be made.

On our Opera House field trips, we were introduced to aspects of construction, including high-tensile steel, and off-the-form concrete perfected by labourers from Italy. In addition to the field trips, I periodically walked to the viewing platform at the Sydney Opera House site. The concrete base of the building was starting to appear like a giant open-air Greek theatre.

I collected all the written material I could find concerning the Opera House—the file of press cuttings alone became several inches thick. One of the most common headings for a news article about the construction was "Blunder." On one front page, the lettering for this word was more than five centimetres (two inches) high. All headlines were designed to catch the public's attention. Here are a few examples:

"Blunder! Govt. loses control of Opera House"

"Behind the Opera House blunder"

"Oops, look what's happened now!"

"The great Opera House controversy"

"The most comic Opera House"

This last heading serves to introduce an extensive body of cartoons. An early example was of a whale in the shape of the building accepting loads of pound notes into the openings of the shell vaults. The caption quoted Dean Ashworth, "We all know that a building today is never built for what you say it is going to cost." That was when the cost estimate was $4 million. In the decade following, it rose first to $50 million, then to more than $100 million.

Not all the cartoons were critical of the project. George Molnar, a member of the architecture faculty at the University of Sydney, strongly supported Jørn Utzon during the continuing controversies at the Opera House. Some of his best cartoons were insightful portrayals of labour strikes, cost overruns and the public's ignorance of the significance of one of the world's great buildings being created at Sydney's front door.

George Molnar was the final-year studio teacher. I was fortunate to attend his design lectures and my admiration for him expanded way beyond his humour in cartoons and cryptic captions. His German education revealed itself in his accent, and I found that he loved the northern parts of Europe as well as Mediterranean countries. He particularly appreciated the architecture of Alvar Aalto in Finland.

"But why have an inside? We'll never use it."

"But why have an inside? We'll never use it." A cartoon by George Molnar, which appeared in the Sydney Morning Herald *in March, 1966. Reproduced with permission.*

Together with other students, I would often watch as he strode back and forth across the quadrangle between the Great Hall and the old Fisher Library. Struck by inspiration, he would suddenly stop and head back to his office. We watched at a distance as he effortlessly drew figures on paper. Then we looked for the result in the following morning's newspaper.

Molnar's ability to come to the essence of an idea with minimal line-work was exemplary. For the cover of an issue of the *Current Affairs Bulletin* he created a symbol of the Opera House: a canary singing in a yellow cage with two hands sheltering it, as if it was under a vaulted ceiling.

Despite the controversy that surrounded the project, Jørn Utzon held to his poetic descriptions of "the dramatic moments" that would connect views of the Opera House roofs from the Sydney Harbour Bridge with patrons' entry to the building and experiences within. His response to media criticism was to speak of the building as a whole. He told of how the shell vaults would tie the spectator's view of the building to the drama produced inside. A building is usually referred to as having four facades— or sides—but Utzon consistently referred to the view of the shell vaults from above as the "fifth facade."

The public was yet to understand what the architect meant by his vision for a building that would "prepare the audience for a festival."

Defending the Opera House

Before leaving the University of Sydney, I sat the final examinations for the Bachelor of Architecture degree. The venue was the Great Hall of the university, and we sat beneath the hammer beam trusses replicated from Cambridge in England.

The last examination was in professional practice and as I entered the Great Hall, I noticed an advertisement pinned to the door. It was for a job of six months' duration. The heading was "Sydney Opera House: Researcher and Official Guide." I wrote down the telephone number and called it after the examination.

At the interview, concern was expressed that media criticism had reached an all-time high. The Stage One platform was completed and a fabrication plant for casting the sections of the shell vaults was in production on site. Stage Two—the erection of these vault segments—had not yet begun. Even though the technology and its applications to construction were new to the world, it was seen as yet another delay in the project and as evidence of further incompetence on the part of the government's leadership.

Then the stage director for the Royal Opera House in Covent Gardens arrived from London. At the time, anyone with opera or theatre production credentials was met at Sydney airport and offered a microphone to comment on the Opera House. There followed another scathing criticism, which was duly published.

The New South Wales government public relations committee decided it was time to stop the deluge of misinformation. They hurriedly composed the advertisement I had seen at the entrance of the Great Hall. To avoid any apparent conflict of interest, it was decided that the engineer, Ove Arup, would pay the salary for the position, but the person appointed would work closely with the government committee and with Jørn Utzon.

I was offered the position. It was an honour to have my first post-graduation job in research and public relations—especially at the Sydney Opera House. I began by studying the backstage dimensions of all major opera houses around the world. This type of objective information was important to make comparisons with Sydney's project. Then there was a need to know what the completed building would be like—and who better to tell of this than Jørn Utzon.

The state government's idea proved to be a good one. Newspaper and magazine readers, radio listeners and television viewers were hungry for objective information about the project from a third-party source. There was also the opportunity to guide dignitaries and the public on the building site in construction downtime.

Four public tours each weekday for the next few months were quickly filled, and I found myself becoming the mouthpiece for the project. In addition to objective information, there was the opportunity to share the anticipated experiences of patrons who would visit the completed building. My descriptions of the spatial sequences from arrival at the ceremonial stairs to being seated in one of the auditoria were directly obtained from conversations with Jørn Utzon. I came to appreciate both his creativity and passion.

Scandinavia calls us

The influence of university teachers who encouraged travel, combined with my experience with Utzon's Opera House project, made it important to look for work abroad. So, my wife Norene and I made definite plans to go to Europe by ship at the end of my term in the Opera House position and gain architectural experience in Scandinavia.

I heard from architectural associates that the ambassador from Denmark was returning to his homeland on the same ship on which we were booked. The long journey was likely to provide opportunities to make his acquaintance, and I was hopeful he might provide contacts in Denmark.

A group of 12 family and friends crowded into our cabin—cabin 417—on the Italian ship *Fair Sky* on June 4, 1963. Then all visitors were required to return to shore, and we held on to streamers as the ship slowly moved from the wharf. Norene and I stayed outside for the few minutes it took to leave Circular Quay and sail past the monumental base of the Sydney Opera House. Then we turned our backs on the lights of Sydney Harbour and went to dinner.

Ships coming to Australia in the 1960s were crowded with immigrants, but the return itinerary to Europe was more like an early version of a cruise ship. The report from my associates that the ambassador from Denmark would be on the *Fair Sky* proved true. We met the honourable gentleman playing quoits on the upper deck. His friendship with Jørn Utzon, my work at the Opera House and my interest in working for an architect in Denmark were reason enough for good conversations.

Five weeks later, we arrived at Naples and boarded a train bound for Paris. A Renault car with tourist plates was awaiting our arrival. For three months, we camped in central and southern Europe. Then we began to see signs that summer was beginning to end. We noticed this particularly as we collected our daily supply of fruit and vegetables at the open-air markets. We knew winter was coming, but our lack of experience made us unaware of the time when it would reach the northern reaches of Europe. We started to drive north, through Switzerland, to the East German border.

At this border, the customs official seemed interested in a portfolio of architectural drawings, which were kept beneath our belongings in the back of the Renault. The array of plans, sections, elevations and perspectives was placed against a fence and scrutinised as if they represented some future incursion of modern architecture into the Soviet bloc.

Fortunately, they returned them to us—which was important. The architectural portfolio was intended to enable me to find work in an architectural office in Denmark. Danish design was recognised for its leadership in the 1950s and into the 60s. But Sweden was already overtaking it.

We crossed on a ferry to Gedser in southern Denmark and, as darkness fell, we found a deserted campground. The proprietor was surprised to see us the next morning—perhaps because of the cold temperature—but he dutifully collected the fee. We continued north to Copenhagen.

We decided that the first point of call would be the office of the Danish Society of Architects to obtain a list of architectural offices in Copenhagen. In response to my inquiries, the secretary told me what I already knew. Obtaining work with an architect in Denmark would be difficult—many foreign architects were wanting the experience. There was also a shortage of apartments in Copenhagen. The secretary concluded her appraisal of conditions not being favourable to foreign architects with a reference to the cost of car registration in Denmark.

It was all just as we had been told. I returned to the car and shared a report of the conversation with Norene. Suddenly, what we had thought to be our journey's end was superseded by the idea that perhaps Sweden—and Stockholm in particular—was our new destination. We had been in Copenhagen for only a couple of hours. We conferenced for a few minutes and pointed the car in the direction of Sweden.

It was not that we expected that finding work in an architect's office in Stockholm would be easy. Or that housing would be more attainable, or less expensive. As we discussed our options, it simply felt good that Stockholm would be our home.

It was already late in the day when we crossed by ferry from Helsingor, Denmark, to Halsingborg, Sweden. Then we drove through the night the 560 kilometres (350 miles) from the ferry crossing to Stockholm. The new day was Friday, October 4, and we celebrated our arrival in Stockholm by staying at a hotel in the city centre. Camping was over—for now.

It was time to prepare for winter and work. That meant finding an apartment and the right architect's office. But that agenda must wait until after Sabbath. We carried a couple of bags into the hotel room, commented on how wonderful it was to be in the security of Scandinavia, then sighed, showered and slept.

The next morning, we confirmed at the hotel reception how to find our way to the *Adventkyrkan*—the Stockholm Seventh-day Adventist Church. It was not far away, but it was more comfortable to drive, using the car that had become so familiar to us during the past three months.

We were welcomed at the door of the church, and almost immediately an American couple introduced themselves and invited us to sit with them. Sitting together also allowed us to benefit from the Swedish church member who translated the texts and sermon into English during the service.

Our new American friends, Dr "Reggie" Register and his wife Helen from Loma Linda University, California, graciously invited us to their apartment for lunch. We followed them across the bridge to the island of Lidingo and entered the second floor of what appeared to be a single-family dwelling. We learned that they had rented the second floor of the house for the duration of the academic year and that the owners were out of town for a few weeks. After our long journey, it was wonderful to relax in the luxury of a Swedish home with English-speaking hosts.

Then they shocked us with an invitation.

"You should come and stay with us," they said. "There's a small apartment in the attic. It will be fine with the owners."

We felt it would be the height of indecency to move into a house when we had not met the owners, and it seemed to us to be audacious for the renters to offer the owner's attic apartment. We thanked Reggie and Helen for their kind offer and we declined.

But that night our car was broken into, and we were left with only a portfolio of architectural drawings and the clothes we had taken to the hotel room. We thought the better of the Registers' offer.

The invitation to drop in anytime was acted on that first Sunday morning in Stockholm. We simply said, "If the offer to stay in the apartment upstairs is still open, we'd like to accept it." The explanation was simple, as was the move in. We had little to carry up the stairs.

Two activities occupied the next two weeks. One was apartment hunting; the other was job hunting.

Real estate rentals were no more available in Stockholm than in Copenhagen, but we were told that the design and comfort standards were so high that we could accept an apartment on the telephone, sight unseen. We did not get the opportunity to test this, however, for there was always a long waiting list. We were serious about apartment hunting for we did not want to impose unduly on Reggie and Helen's hospitality or their vacationing landlord.

Finally, we found a small *stuga*—a cabin—in a forest. It was a red wooden summer cottage, with a hand-operated water pump looking like a piece of sculpture in the front yard. There were no other landscape elements except the surrounding pine forest. Posters of dangerous mushrooms hung in the entry porch, but there were no mushrooms in sight. It was now mid-October and the locals spoke of the approaching winter. We had already noticed that the days were growing shorter.

With our accommodation settled for the time, we could focus on job hunting. Our *stuga* was located on a spur of the Stockholm archipelago, quite a distance from the city. That meant our little Renault tracked back and forth each day as I took my portfolio of drawings to a select group of architectural offices.

A book on new Swedish architecture provided the basis for investigating the work of leading architects. Each day, I would select an architect, then Norene and I would visit some examples of the architect's work, obtain the address of their office from the Swedish Society of Architects, and find our way to the office doorstep.

I soon discovered that there was quite a group of foreign architects wanting to work in Stockholm. They also carried portfolios of their design work, and I began to recognise familiar faces as we met on the way in or out of architects' offices.

It did not much matter who was coming or going. If the office had work and needed help, their space was filled quickly. If there was insufficient work on the drawing boards, the principal architect had better things to do than interview.

It was a discouraging few weeks and we began to consider abandoning the Scandinavian dream and heading for London.

Help finding work in Sweden

Then we met Herbert Blomstedt. He had been conducting the Oslo Philharmonic Orchestra in the Soviet Union. Already highly recognised, he travelled extensively as a guest conductor to orchestras in Europe. Home for the weekend, he attended the Stockholm Adventist Church where we were introduced.

"So, you're an architect from Australia," he said. "Do you know Jørn Utzon?"

He followed my affirmative answer with a second question.

"You want to work for an architect in Stockholm?"

"Yes, indeed!"

"Would the office of Gösta Åbergh be of interest?"

Gösta Åbergh!

Before I had time to swallow, he went on to tell how, as principal conductor of the Oslo Philharmonic Orchestra, he had participated in approving the competition conditions for the design of a new concert hall in Norway's capital. It was an architectural competition for Scandinavian architects held at approximately the same time as the competition for the Sydney Opera House design. The Oslo project had been shelved for several years so that issues of a small triangular site and funding could be addressed. Now the project had been given the green light. As a member of the competition jury, Maestro Blomstedt knew the architect who had won first prize—Gösta Åbergh.

"I will telephone Gösta on Monday morning and mention that I met you. You should telephone him around two o'clock Monday afternoon."

He handed me a telephone number. And he was gone.

The next day was spent visiting the recent work of the Åbergh Arkitektkontor—Gösta Åbergh's practice office. It was not only an office I wanted to join—I was excited by the possibility of working on another major cultural commission obtained through competition.

I telephoned Gösta as recommended and he invited me to come and visit. The office address he gave brought me to a lake at Sköndal. A large white 18th-century house—the family home—was close to the lake. A short distance away was a 17th-century red wooden two-storey building. On the ground floor was a reception space, Gösta's office, a meeting room and a small woodshop for making models. There were four rooms upstairs. Each accommodated the workplaces of two architects.

As I entered the reception area, Gösta came to meet me and repeated Herbert Blomstedt's words.

"Hello," he said. "You're from Australia. Do you know Jørn Utzon?"

Well, yes, I did. I told him briefly of my work at the Sydney Opera House and the discussions I had had with Utzon. We talked for a while, then I opened my portfolio. He scanned through it, then took me to the one free space upstairs. There I met Ole, a Norwegian architect. We shook hands.

I was hired! Ole's workplace—now also mine—had a window to the lake.

The Registers brought more good news to church the following weekend—a potential lead in our quest for accommodation. They told us of a Swedish couple who were friends with one of their colleagues in the United States. We were taken to their friends' home for a social visit and before we left, this couple had opened both their hearts and their attic to us. The attic apartment had a small living space, bedroom and bath. We would share their kitchen.

The offer was well timed—the summer *stuga* in the pine forest was not suitable for habitation in winter. We moved out as the first heavy snow began to fall. Better yet, our new home was not far from the design office where I would work, and Norene could now begin a serious search for work as a physiotherapist at a regional hospital.

By the end of November, we had both settled into work. Our little Renault provided transportation from our apartment to the railway station where Norene caught a train to the hospital, then I drove along country roads to Gösta Åbergh's office on the lake. Life was good.

We saw the daylight hours shrink as the Christmas season approached and we enjoyed the snow, even if there were moments when our small car proved to be more of a sled than expected.

A "strange guy" who changed our lives

Our appreciation for the company of Reggie and Helen continued to grow, and we became comfortable dropping in to see them whenever we chose to take a drive to the island of Lidingo. One Sunday afternoon in January, our visit to the Registers coincided with that of another couple, the Wallers. They were from Oklahoma and current residents of the Wenigren Center, a community of academics spending a year in research at Stockholm. Professor Waller was a biochemist.

When I was introduced as an architect, Professor Waller mentioned that an American architect and his wife were also living in the Wenigren Center.

"He's from Ohio State. A strange guy."

The architecture conversation stopped when it was discovered that we shared an interest in classical music. Professor Waller focused on this.

"There's a string quartet concert at the Wenigren Center in a week or two. Would you like to come?"

We would. And did.

During the concert interval, Professor Waller pointed out the professor of architecture from Ohio State University. His name was Perry Borchers. We were invited to his apartment after the concert and while his wife, Myra, organised refreshments, Perry took me to his study and put a stereoscope in front of me. This optical instrument has two lenses for viewing pairs of photographs—the left eye sees a picture that is taken to the left of one that is seen by the right eye. The brain does the rest and provides a spatial (three-dimensional) model of what was photographed—in this case impressive interiors of Baroque architecture. I found all the spatial models to be exciting, and my response must have been in sharp contrast to the average visitor to the Borchers' apartment— and definitely more supportive than the response from a certain biochemist.

I found Perry Borchers to be a precise academic and an architect with a passion for research in photogrammetry—the science of obtaining measurements from three-dimensional models of space.

Time passed quickly. Weeks turned into months, and winter to spring. Norene and I made travel plans for the summer. We would drive north through Norway, cross from the North Cape to Finland, drive down to Helsinki and on through the Soviet Union to Vienna. We would camp, and we obtained the necessary permissions from Intourist—the official tourist office in the Soviet Union—to do so.

In general, our travel eventuated according to plan. However, we were delayed for a week in Hammerfest, Norway, due to a collision we had with a truck on the crest of the narrow road. We were towed into Hammerfest and had to wait until the Norwegian coastal ship *Hurtigruten* brought spare parts for the Renault.

Fortunately, we were able to adjust the times of the permit to stay in campgrounds in the Soviet Union. Our last night in the West was within sight of the border towers. Then we crossed and headed for Leningrad.

We had a problem a few days later. We were camping in a Moscow campground, and our little tent seemed rather vulnerable in protecting our few valuables while we went sightseeing. We chose to place our better clothes, slides, books and Norene's souvenir Swedish folk dress underneath the seats of the car. We parked in Marx Prospckt and thought we had successfully exchanged greetings with the policeman directing traffic. Then we visited the Kremlin. When we returned, the policeman was still there. Our valuables were not.

The policeman assisted in directing us to the police station. There we were told we must be mistaken.

"There is no crime in the Soviet Union."

We eventually resorted to contacting the Australian Embassy and received a statement to the effect that it was reported to them that our belongings were stolen. It was a useful document when we later filed a claim with our insurance company.

The delay of several days waiting for a report of the theft needed to be reported to Intourist, and we received new dates for staying at campgrounds between Moscow, Minsk and Smolensk on the way to the Polish border. We enjoyed our travels, although we discovered a problem after arriving at the Poland–Czechoslovakia border. Due to the delays, our visa to Czechoslovakia, as it was known in those days, had expired. We had to return to Warsaw and wait through a public holiday to apply for a new visa. Then we found we could only obtain a transit visa to cross Czechoslovakia in no more than 24 hours. That is what we did.

We arrived in Vienna in the early hours of Friday, August 15, 1964. The date was significant, but we did not know that yet.

On arrival, we parked our car outside the American Express office and waited for it to open at 9 am. In the 1960s, the American Express office would hold mail until it was collected, so before our summer's travels we had given the address of the Vienna office to those with whom we were in correspondence. We were eager to hear news—particularly from our parents in Australia.

We collected quite a stack of mail. One envelope was longer than the rest and was completely unexpected. It carried the logo of Ohio State University. We opened it and read its message in disbelief. On the recommendation of Professor Perry Borchers, I was offered a teaching position for two years. The director of the School of Architecture and Landscape Architecture outlined that I would teach in the first-year design studio and supervise fifth-year thesis projects. Our surprise was heightened by the concluding line:

"This offer will be held for you until August 15, 1964."

That day! A significant day, indeed.

Norene and I headed for the hills above Vienna. We re-read the Ohio State letter and read our mail from Australia. We thought and we prayed. Then we found an office where we could send a telegram of acceptance.

The Ohio State University is a Land Grant institution, which meant that salaries were paid only to those who had taken the American oath of allegiance. Accordingly, we decided to go to the American Embassy in Munich—our next destination after Vienna. The officer there slowed us down.

"Do you realise what this means to you?" he asked. "You will be giving up your Australian rights!"

Perhaps we had been a bit hasty in our request to take the oath of allegiance. The officer phoned the British Embassy, and the call reinforced the notion that we were making a mistake. A further telephone call, this time to the Australian Embassy, led to a clearly recognisable Australian accent on the speaker phone.

When asked about the oath of allegiance and loss of citizenship, he replied to the American officer: "No sweat, mate! We'll take them back."

I repeated the oath of allegiance and felt good about it. I also thought how wonderful it was that I would teach and be paid.

Living the dream

That letter changed our plans and our lives. Our work experience in Sweden was over. Within days, we took our Renault back to Paris and sold it, purchased air tickets from Luxemburg to New York, and arrived at the Idlewild (now John F Kennedy) airport. After clearing customs, we stepped on board a bus and asked the driver how much it would cost to buy a ticket. We were immediately attracted by the driver's response to our question.

"Man, I loves the way you talk," he said. As if we had an accent!

We visited used car dealers along New York's Broadway in Manhattan and purchased a 1962 Chevy Corvair. The car proved to be a good investment and served us well for almost two years. After visiting the 1964 World's Fair at Flushing, we set off on our drive to Columbus, Ohio. In keeping with our reputation for not taking the shortest route, we drove through upstate New York to the Niagara Falls, across Ontario to Detroit and into Ohio.

We found a small apartment on the edge of the Ohio State University campus and went to visit Director Elliot Whitaker at the School of Architecture and Landscape Architecture. We were expressing our appreciation for his letter when he interrupted with a request.

"Can you both come to a lecture on Thursday night? We have Felix Candela coming to speak, but there are not many students and faculty here this week. I'd like you to come."

Of course we would. I would have gladly listened to a lecture from Mexico's master of constructing thin concrete shells, even if the director had not asked it as a favour. Felix Candela had perfected the technology for building roofs to churches and market halls in Mexico. Jørn Utzon had originally thought that the shells of the Sydney Opera House could be poured in that way, but the scale was too large.

We arrived early for the lecture. A small audience was gathering, and I noticed that Director Whitaker and his wife were seated several rows in front of us. He turned around, saw us and spoke in a rather loud voice.

"Oh, Neville, I had a phone call today from Harvard University. They want you to give a lecture."

My one conversation with the director had not given evidence of a sense of humour, but I reckoned it must certainly exist, so I laughed. But the reference to Harvard proved to have no undertone of humour, for after the lecture I discovered that the invitation was serious.

While we were planning our summer travels, Perry Borchers had written to Elliot Whitaker indicating that he thought I was a good candidate for the first Master of Architecture degree from Ohio State. The program was a year away from final approval, so he planted the idea of offering a teaching position to this young Australian architect for the coming academic year. Teaching could continue for a second year while I took graduate courses in photogrammetry and worked on projects recording historic architecture across the eastern half of the United States.

This much was understandable, for I knew that the director had responded positively to Professor Borchers. Our presence on campus was evidence of that. But there was more.

While Director Whitaker was arranging visa approval for me to come to the United States to teach, a circular letter from the Harvard Graduate School of Design arrived on his desk. It inquired if there were any faculty who might be considered for inclusion in Harvard's visiting lecture series for 1964–65.

Professor Borcher's reference to my association with Jørn Utzon on the Sydney Opera House seemed reason enough to suggest that I might be able to give an interesting lecture.

The director submitted my name.

With Harvard now having selected the speakers for its lecture series, I was told that I could take two weeks leave from teaching in February so Norene and I could drive to Boston, with visits to Cornell and Syracuse Universities on the way.

In the Fall semester, as I taught in studio and enrolled in some master's-level classes at Ohio State, my mind assembled the content for the Harvard lecture. There was the cultural history of Australia and how Jørn Utzon approached the international competition with poetic licence. I was certainly privileged to know the architect. There was the expertise of engineer Ove Arup, who was able to take the pencil lines on Utzon's elevations and make sense of them. Then there was the problem of how to build the concrete shells, and the creative relationship between architect and engineer that was needed in finding the solution.

Into the lecture I could weave the politics of the New South Wales government and how elections were won and lost. The public had no use for an Opera House when the beaches were much more to their liking. And the lecture could include cartoons by George Molnar. His incisive lines and insightful commentary provided humour to a serious undertaking.

The weather cooperated as Norene and I drove on the northern route to the East Coast. We felt privileged to be granted the opportunity to drive onto the Harvard campus, live in a room on the top floor of the faculty club and visit the office and most recent work of Jose Luis Sert, Harvard's dean of architecture. He took me on a tour of Boston, spending extended time at his recently completed MIT Student Union building. This was the royal treatment that Director Whitaker at Ohio State had organised, and it included dining at the faculty club for all meals.

The day came for the lecture. It was a Thursday evening event. We met the organiser of the lecture series for dinner and were hardly surprised to hear that, at 24, I was the youngest architect to ever participate.

The lecture on Sydney's new Opera House went well, as did the question-and-answer session. Late that night, Norene and I walked back to the faculty club, climbed the stairs to our room, and felt that we needed to pinch ourselves to be sure it was all true. Then the telephone rang.

The caller began, "I understand you have just given a lecture on the Sydney Opera House at the Graduate School of Design. I'm calling from Yale. Could you possibly give the lecture here?"

So we went to Yale University, and visited Paul Rudolf's new architecture building and Louis Kahn's art museum. The lecture was scheduled for the noon hour, so it could be well attended at short notice. The Sydney Opera House was again centre stage in my life.

Later, as we drove along the turnpike back towards Columbus, Ohio, Norene and I reflected on the Lord's leading in our lives and how incredible it was for us to benefit from the educational opportunities in the United States of America. The experiences reinforced the role of mentors. Architect Jørn Utzon would never know how his poetic descriptions of a building "to prepare the audience for a festival" would stay with me and guide me. George Molnar's humour in cartoons and commentaries had enriched the compass of my life. Professor Perry Borchers' initiative in recommending me to his director had opened opportunities to me I would not have dreamed possible.

But there is more than that. I could never be convinced otherwise than that there was a plan for my life—a plan larger than I could draw.

---

1 Cited in Ove Arup, "Sydney Opera House," *Architectural Design*, 3, March 1965, page 135.

2

EUROPE

There were two faculty members in the Department of Architecture at the University of Sydney who influenced me in significant ways. Both shared a connection to the European architecture and art scene.

George Molnar was the fifth-year studio master. His lectures were remarkable analyses of design problems. At the conclusion of each lecture, the blackboard was a record in yellow chalk of where his thoughts and heavy German accent had taken us. Molnar's outstanding draftsmanship was also seen in his cartoons. Readers of the *Sydney Morning Herald* enjoyed his drawings and incisive comments. Minimal lines described men and women from any country or setting. I appreciated his humour.

Lloyd Rees was one of Australia's great landscape artists and it was incredible to have this master of landscape painting as a tutor during my university years. In the early years of our program, he encouraged students to sketch outdoors—a habit I was pleased to acquire. But it was in my fifth year, when I sat in his fine arts lectures, that I came to appreciate his profound influence. These lectures were filled with personal stories delivered in a soft voice, while he turned the pages of his sketchbooks. Every drawing was of a favourite place, to which he returned on sabbaticals as often as possible.

It was there that I heard for first time of San Gimignano and other towns in Tuscany. Majorca was another of Rees' favourite locations. It was no wonder that students of that time determined to travel to Europe as soon as they could save funds or complete their cadetship with one of the government offices.

In class one afternoon in November, 1962, Lloyd Rees reported that he had been approached by the headmaster of the Kiama High School, south of Sydney, to paint six large oil paintings for the gymnasium there. It is true that the town of Kiama, and nearby Gerringong, were special places to Rees, and the subjects of many of his paintings. But it was beyond belief that arguably the greatest landscape painter in Australia at the time would be asked to provide paintings for a school gym.

Rees had every reason to say no. Instead, he suggested to the headmaster that he put the idea to his fine arts class as a class project. He invited each student in the class of 30 to submit a sketch proposal. In a class competition, six winners would be selected, and they would then complete a 1.8 × 1.5 metre (6 × 5 feet) oil painting of their proposal.

I was one of the lucky winners selected to bring their sketch to life—no matter that this would be my first oil painting.

Kiama is a coastal town, and my sketch was a landscape view of a knoll with a stand of tall Norfolk pines that overlooked the Pacific Ocean. Other student themes included historical aspects of the town's industry, the Cathedral Rocks geological feature and semi-abstract treatments of surrounding hills. When complete, the six paintings were installed at Kiama High School, with a ceremony that included the students and Lloyd Rees.

It was influences like these, and that of Jørn Utzon, architect of the Sydney Opera House, that made me want to always have a sketchbook handy. Since graduation, it has been my habit to carry a sketchbook with me.

Time to travel

Travel was a given for Norene and me, with the architecture and sights of Europe the natural focus. With limited funds, we planned a combination of camping for three months, then work in an architectural office—ideally in Scandinavia.

Our journey on the Italian ship *Fair Sky* began on June 4, 1963. Ports on the itinerary were Singapore, Colombo, Aden, Port Said and Naples.

There were many wonderful experiences on the Italian ship. We learned to speak some Italian and to cover our bread plate with olive oil for dipping, and we survived several days of monsoons while crossing the Indian Ocean. Each night during bad weather, the captain would commence his evening report with the statement: "This is the captain speaking. I have been a bad driver today." His thick accent made the message seem lighter and the worst days were almost enjoyable.

A large bunch of bananas in cabin 417 after the port of Colombo, Sri Lanka (then Ceylon) also contributed to our enjoyment. We had acquired it from boats coming to the side of the ship.

It was the end of a great day ashore, travelling by train and bus. We stood at the ship's rail, high above the water, and watched a cluster of small boats directly below us. It was the last chance for local merchants to sell their goods to the ship's passengers, and they also needed to change Australian coins for paper money. I felt willing to become involved in the money exchange—we could spend loose change on board the ship.

"Twenty-one shillings to the pound," called the boatman. It was better than 20—the number of shillings in the Australian pound in the currency of those days.

"Twenty-two shillings to the pound."

Time was rapidly closing in on the boatmen, for the anchors would soon be weighed for departure.

"Twenty-three shillings to the pound."

That did seem to be a good deal. But while I was quietly isolating an Australian pound note, the transaction became even better.

"Twenty-three shillings to the pound and a bunch of bananas."

"OK!" I shouted.

A basket was connected to a pulley, and the money and bananas placed inside. It was raised and passed along to me. We emptied the contents and put the pound note in the basket. The merchant took the note and smiled. Then we headed for the open sea.

After Aden, we made an unscheduled stop in Massawa to bring a group of expatriates back to Italy. Conditions in Ethiopia were deteriorating at the time.

As we approached Port Said, Egypt, a one-day excursion to the city of Cairo, its highly regarded museum and the pyramids at Giza was offered to passengers while the ship went through the Suez Canal. We debated whether we should spend some of our savings nest egg on this tour, but we were glad we took the excursion.

The last port of call was Naples. For us, it was the beginning of our European journey. We were fortunate to be able to stay an extra night on board the *Fair Sky* after arriving in port. This gave us the opportunity to carry a very heavy suitcase to the bond store and arrange for its long-term storage. We familiarised ourselves with the city centre and purchased rail tickets from Naples to Rome and on to Paris, after a stop in Visp. The next day, we carried our remaining suitcases from our cabin to the dock, hired a taxi to take us to the train station and settled in for the journey to Rome.

An Italian couple sat opposite us on the train. Their alternating amorous and antagonistic behaviour kept us entertained during the journey. In Rome, we transferred to the Paris train, made a station stop in Milan, then caught a few hours' sleep during the early hours of the morning. We awoke to the mountainous landscape of Switzerland.

As we looked out at the scenery, a cartoon by George Molnar came into my mind. While on a year of sabbatical leave from the University of Sydney, he had sent the drawing and a description as a "Postcard from Abroad" to the *Sydney Morning Herald*. The writing under his cartoon matched my thoughts as we travelled. His view was from the window of a dining carriage. Ours was not.

He wrote:

> The train glides at 60 miles an hour. I am in the dining
> car, looking into the plate-glass shopwindow of the
> world, inspecting mountain peaks on display...
>
> (White clouds hang on mountains like slightly lifted
> ballet skirts. It's a ballet of elephants)...
>
> The level in the bottle measures distances travelled...
>
> (Cows munch around in photogenic groupings,
> advertising national products. Women in the fields,
> ample and round—advertising women.)
>
> The main products of Switzerland are snow, views,
> watches and cheese. Snow and views are quite recent.
> Nobody considered snow anything but a nuisance until
> the late nineteenth century, and views were civilised
> landscapes of rolling hills to fill spaces between figures
> in paintings....Both snow and views were introduced
> to Switzerland by Englishmen who wanted to travel to
> places returning from which even England felt cosy and
> warm. Silver forest of transmission towers. A factory, all
> glass and elegance. Inside they split seconds....
>
> The bottle is empty. This is the end of the journey. I
> wonder where that is?[1]

For us, the destination was Visp. The bottle that we emptied
on the trip was a large one of aerated mineral water. I had noticed
hurrying passengers in the railway station in Rome stop just
long enough to purchase a bottle of water. Thinking they knew
something that we did not, I had followed the routine.

Now it was time for a late breakfast. We lowered our belongings
onto the platform and looked for a shop. We found a bakery and
a store that sold cheese, then sat on our suitcases and ate while
we waited for the train that would take us up the cog railway to
Zermatt.

We stayed awake during the steep rail inclines, and we carried
our suitcases along the main street of Zermatt to the youth hostel

at the other end of town. The view from our hostel window was heavy mist. We could have been anywhere. Then we collapsed onto the bunk beds.

The sleep was good. The next thing we knew, bright sunlight was streaming through the window. We jumped out of bed and there, framed by the window surround, was a picture-postcard view of the Matterhorn. I rushed to grab my camera, half expecting that the view of the spectacular peak would disappear. It was a sight to behold. The black and white mountain thrust itself to a height of 4500 metres (14,750 feet) above sea level and was set majestically against a saturated blue sky.

The weather was ideal all day, and we experienced the enormous splayed forms of rock from different viewpoints as we hiked the trail to Gornergrat, southeast of Zermatt, overlooking the Gorner Glacier. This was a good introduction to Switzerland.

Returning on the cog railway to Visp the following day, we chose a local train to Sion, then a fast ride into France.

Our French adventure

We arrived in Paris early on Friday morning and made our way by Metro to the Renault Auto Delivery Centre. It was here that a grey Renault Gordini awaited us. The red licence plates ended with "TTA75," which indicated to local inhabitants that we were tourists. It was a detail that we would have preferred to avoid communicating. In a couple of days, there would be evidence of the disadvantage.

It took most of the day to arrange the paperwork on the vehicle. Then we sat in the car and accepted that the manual and all the official papers were only in French, which we could not read. Doing the best we could, we headed into peak-hour traffic, travelling on the right-hand side of the road—which, for us, was the wrong side.

We approached our first roundabout in our shiny new car. Citroens flashed by, observing a social distance that was closer than we wanted, and it was at this point that Norene and I decided on our roles without discussion.

I would manoeuvre the vehicle around the circle a first time, while Norene checked the exit possibilities. By the time I had completed the second circuit, she would know which sign, in French, was the one we should follow, and I would position the car to take the exit the third time around. It was slow but thorough, and eventually our teamwork brought us to the courtyard of Pur Aliment, a health food company.

This was an important address for several reasons. Many years before, Norene's father had travelled in Europe on Sanitarium Health Food Company business, and before we left Australia, we had promised to bring his greetings to the director of Pur Aliment. Monsieur Kiehl was his name. We recognised that a visit to a health food supply centre might be just what was needed before the weekend. Furthermore, Monsieur Kiehl might be able to assist us in locating a store where we could purchase a pup tent—a type of small A-frame tent that was common at the time—so we could camp while travelling.

On all counts, the visit was successful. It began with me taking Norene to the side of a Citroen Goddess that was parked in the courtyard. Next to it was a red MGB. My quiet commentary on the beautiful Citroen was interrupted by a voice with a definite French accent.

"Ah! Isn't it *magnifique!*"

We shook hands with Monsieur Kiehl. He wanted to tell us more about his car—and he did. The couple had recently returned from their summer vacation.

"We usually go to Bordeaux. It's good! This year we went to Lisbon," he explained. Then added, "I drove the Citroen. My wife, she drove the MGB."

Perhaps our confusion showed on our faces, for he then assured us that he and his wife arranged to meet in certain towns for lunch and dinner, and they stayed together at the same hotel. We thought this was an interesting introduction to France.

We were given armfuls of fresh bread, peanut butter, apricot jam and some other jars. All gratis! Then came the reprimand.

"You cannot live in a tent!"

Just then Madam Kiehl arrived. On hearing the point of view expressed by her husband, she joined in. Norene and I assured our hosts that we certainly were going to camp, and all we were asking was if they knew where we could buy a tent. Seeing our determination, Madam Kiehl conceded that she had seen quite large and—presumably somewhat comfortable—tents. In any event, Monsieur Kiehl was anxious to take us for a ride in the Goddess.

We purchased a 2 × 1 metre (6 × 3 feet) pup tent, returned to Pur Aliment, and were then piloted to the camping ground at the Bois de Bologne. We thanked the Kiehls and prepared for Sabbath.

A day of rest is just what created beings need. Whether it is life on the fast track through work, or the schedules we set for ourselves on vacation, we need the Sabbath. It was a delightful day in the woods.

Neville and Norene Clouten camping in the pup tent near Arezzo, Italy in July, 1963.

On Sunday morning, Norene awoke with puffy cheeks and a fever, and she self-diagnosed this to be the mumps. She would not hear of a doctor—she knew the symptoms—and simply announced that our tent would be her isolation ward. As a facile way of getting me out of the picture, she suggested that I visit some architectural sites. The work of Le Corbusier at Cite Universitaire came to my mind.

I folded the map of Paris to the appropriate section, placed it on the passenger seat of the Renault Gordini and drove out of the Bois de Bologne. Everything was going well—almost too well. I was musing on this when a traffic light turned red, and I dutifully stopped.

I noticed a *gendarme* (police officer) on the pavement, but I did not anticipate that he would open the passenger door and climb in beside me. He spoke to me in rapid French, and when the light turned green, signalled I that should drive on. He kept talking and accompanied his speech by pointing his white baton as he directed me. I guessed he was on a call to an accident or other emergency and that I was the first car on the scene that Sunday morning.

After many traffic lights and turns—left and right—we were driving in a residential area. His voice was a continuous rise and fall, accompanied by the pointing baton movements. Then he spoke a word I understood.

"Halt!"

He was ready to alight as I pulled to the kerb.

"*Merci, monsieur*," he said, and headed for the front door of his home—and presumably morning coffee.

The experience reminded me that we were tourists and that the "TTA75" at the end of the licence plate signalled the fact. I tried to avoid the thought of putting my foot on the accelerator every time I heard the whistle of a *gendarme*.

Paris is a wonderful city, and my love for it has grown through many subsequent visits.

Norene's recovery from the mumps after six days signalled that it was time to leave the Bois de Bologne. She seemed particularly pleased that my interest in seeing some important new examples of Le Corbusier's architecture would take us to the east, towards Switzerland.

Further travels in Europe

On our way, we visited several concrete bridges by the Swiss engineer Robert Maillart. One or two examples were difficult to locate, but all were incredibly elegant. The bridge detours led us to Bern, famous for its bears and boutiques. Our visit to the bear pit was not expensive and it began a long-term fascination and love for bears—brown, black and polar.

Seven years after our first visit to Bern, and with the influence of the equivalent Scandinavian word for bear, we named our firstborn son Bjorn.

Norene and I travelled in our Renault with all manner of art and architecture agendas. The pilgrimage chapel by Le Corbusier at Ronchamps beckoned us back to France. We camped near the border with Switzerland, and the next morning we joined a

Neville and Norene Clouten enjoying lunch at Zurich Water Storage in July, 1963.

group of architects from around the world who were making their way up the path to the chapel. It was a great experience to walk around and through this magnificent piece of sculpture, enjoying the forms and spaces, its focused areas of primary colours and use of dramatic lighting. After a description of Ronchamps, my diary reads, "On the way back to Bern..."

It was becoming clear to me that Norene had decided Switzerland was her favourite European country, and, as navigator, she was in a position to accomplish many return visits.

Actually, Switzerland seemed to open its heart to us. We visited its lakes, towns and mountains, and we found wonderful camping grounds. This continued as we travelled into northern Italy. We crisscrossed southern Europe down to Mount Vesuvius and Naples.

We picked up the large suitcase at the bond store in Naples, unpacked its contents and somehow made them fit into the car. Then we travelled along the coast to Tuscany, making special stops at Sienna and San Gimignano. I was living out the lectures of my art teacher.

By the time we had circled the Italian and French Rivieras and explored Spain, there were signs that summer was beginning to end. We saw this particularly as we collected our daily supply of fruit and vegetables at open-air markets in Portugal. The uniformly plump bunches of grapes we had come to appreciate were now a mixture of purple delicacies. We liked them even more—plucking the full grapes from the bottom of the bunch and sun-ripened raisins from the top.

The markets reflected the change in the seasons beautifully, and about this time, I re-read the following description from our travel guide to Venice, a book which served us well while visiting there. The description is of the Rialto market, but the words easily cross the borders into other European countries.

> In a land still suspicious... of the horrors of deep-frozen, packaged foods, the market stalls record the procession of the seasons. Early in the year they are bright with

great piles of Sicilian oranges and tangerines, apples of an unnatural rosiness, giant hands of bananas, long yellow pears, plump white cauliflowers and the richly striped red and yellow Treviso lettuces. Greeny-purple artichokes and blanched fennel roots in winter and early spring gradually give way to enormous succulent white sticks of Bassano asparagus…and the first gleaming jewel-like cherries. Then come the strawberries, big and small, scenting the air with their peculiar fragrance, golden plums called *gocche d'oro* (drops of gold), the first white-centred peaches, green figs and rough-skinned melons. High summer brings the rather over-large yellow peaches, great green melons red and black inside (better material for the painter than the gourmet), smooth aubergines, stocky green zucchini with their yellow flowers, flame-red tomatoes, the myriad varieties of fungus and piles of green and black grapes. The first pears herald the approach of autumn which comes in with piles of walnuts, dusty brown chestnuts and great luminous orange-red persimmons.…In December strings of hazelnuts and dried figs festoon the stalls. The first sharp mandarin tangerines arrive from Sicily with green leaves still clinging to them and the procession of the Venetian seasons begins again.[2]

New friends and new dreams

Our recognition of the seasonal change made us aware that winter would soon be on the calendar. We slowly began the drive north, stopping at the prehistoric caves of Altimira, Spain, and Lascaux, France. Then we took a route through Switzerland.

A return visit to Sion coincided with one of the final presentations of the Son et Lumiere (a sound and light spectacle). Late at night, we sat on the rocks between the city's Cathedral of Notre Dame de Valere and the Chateau of Tourbillon for the dramatic presentation. Then we retired to our nearby tent.

By now, Norene and I had taken camping to an art form. We would arrive at a camp site and select a small area of grass—next to some form of vegetation, if possible. While I pitched the tent, Norene would put potatoes, cauliflower and whatever other vegetables we had found at the market into our pressure cooker. This sat over, and precariously overhung, the single burner of a gas cylinder.

Often, we found better campsites outside of the community campgrounds. Late one afternoon, we were on the road from Bern to Schüpfheim, where we were intending to camp. As we rounded a curve on the mountain road, our eyes focused on a stand of pine trees not far from a farmhouse. Perhaps the sight brought back memories of the pine forest of the Watagan Mountains outside of Newcastle, Australia. In any event, we turned onto the grassy drive that led to the farmhouse. We approached the farmer in the field and tried to ask permission to camp under the pines. However, he took us to the door of the house to meet his wife. We were invited in, and as we sat around the wooden table in the kitchen, we wrote some words and drew pictures on a sheet of paper.

The farmer wrote, "*Familie* Frederick," and to the best of our understanding, he described their son, who was in the Swiss army, and daughter, who lived in another town. My main contribution was to draw a picture of a small tent and write, "Camping."

I realised that the need to communicate our request to the German-speaking farmer was becoming more pressing, for I could see through the kitchen window that dark clouds were assembling themselves and preparing for action. Then Frau Frederick made an invitation that was perfectly clear. She took Norene by the hand and they climbed a flight of wooden stairs. I followed. There was a bed with a huge comforter and it was clear that it was for us.

We brought in a bag from the car and sat down again at the kitchen table. We were relaxed and ready to enjoy a supper of fresh bread, cheese and honey. What a delightful family!

We retired, and the next sound I heard was the ringing of cowbells. I went downstairs and entered the barn which was attached to the farmhouse. Herr Frederick welcomed me with a German greeting and smile.

I realised that it was not yet 4 am, but I watched the milking process with interest. When it was completed, we left the barn and stood outside. The sunlight was burning away the mist, leaving a crystal-clear sky. I thrilled at the panoramic view. Unable to express my feelings, I tried to put a few pseudo-German words together in the hope of saying, "What a wonderful view!"

Reflecting on what happened next, I think the farmer must have thought I said, "Where is the view?"

He beckoned me to follow, and we walked down the autumn-green field to where the slope changed from gentle grazing land to an escarpment. A wooden shed was right at this point of change in the landscape. The farmer opened the door, and we entered a dark room with a few hand tools scattered around. At the far end, he brushed aside some cobwebs and flung open the shutters. There, framed by the darkness, was a view of a spectacular mountain peak set against the blue sky.

He smiled as if to say, "You asked about a view?"

It seemed to me that the farmer had shared with me a special place of refuge. Perhaps it provided him space for his most personal reflections on life. A place for solitude and silence can do that. I felt privileged to share this experience with the farmer and have often thought of it.

Our camping experiences in 1963 culminated in reaching Scandinavia, then living and working in Stockholm. But the pup tent and gas cylinder were not ready to be retired. In later years, several opportunities took us back to Europe. On one occasion, camping beside fjords along the coast of Norway, I recall the sight of a cruise ship seen from between the flaps of our tent. For a moment, I wondered what that form of luxury would be like.

Little did we know that it would become a reality for us. And not just one cruise. It began in 2004.

Life on a cruise ship

As I contemplated retirement, the possibility of teaching watercolour art on cruise ships seemed to be a good idea. As I explored some options, I found that the Cunard Line offered a theme cruise called "Festival of the Arts" on one of the autumn crossings of the *Queen Elizabeth 2* from Southampton to New York.

I telephoned Cunard and the conversation went something like:

"I'm impressed with the many forms of the arts that are included in the festival theme cruise—big band concerts, lectures, a string quartet...What about a watercolour workshop?"

The reply gave me confidence: "We would, if we had someone to teach it."

So it was agreed. The Cunard office arranged that Norene and I would have a cabin in the entertainment section of the *QE2*, and an honorarium would cover the purchase of good quality paper, brushes and watercolour tubes.

I asked my contact at Cunard: "How many patrons do you think will come?"

The reply was: "A dozen—perhaps 15 to 18."

My preparation for the workshop was to make black-and-white copies on watercolour paper of a sketch from one of my sketchbooks. The sketches were mostly accurate records of buildings and towns, though some moments of relaxation had inspired me to be more impressionistic.

The sketch that I copied for the cruise workshop was of Stonehenge. It seemed appropriate, in that the *QE2* was sailing from Southampton—a port not far from the historic site on England's Salisbury Plains.

The workshop venue was the elegant Queen Elizabeth room at 10 am each morning of the cruise.

On the first day, Norene and I came early and squeezed small blobs of four colours onto china plates. I placed the brushes on a demonstration table, and we waited for the maximum of 18 patrons. Eighty came.

For the next two hours, I demonstrated a sky wash to successive groups who gathered around me. Then each participant picked up a brush and joined the chaos that otherwise filled the room. Such a diverse family of paintings as those that came into being over the next few days has rarely been assembled on either side of the Atlantic.

The greatest surprise was at the conclusion of the first morning's workshop. After waiting and bartering for a brush, these kind patrons commended me for the structure of the workshop. They said they were really enjoying the event. When I stepped off the ship in New York, I was ready to exchange computer keyboards for brushes dipped into paint. I knew I had found my retirement career.

The first workshop with the Cunard Line led to others. The new *Queen Mary 2* was launched in 2004 and I was invited to teach on the "Three Continents Cruise." The supply of art materials had been streamlined since the first workshop. There were now watercolour kits that included good quality paper, paints, brushes and odds and ends. Patrons signed their name to receive a kit at a nominal charge.

The starting point for the "Three Continents Cruise" was Fort Lauderdale, Florida. After two days of cruising, we arrived at Bridgetown, Barbados. I noticed a table with a sign, "Vantage Deluxe World Travel." As I began the walk back to the ship after a day ashore in Bridgetown, I heard my name. The two Vantage representatives must have heard about me from some of the "Three Continents Cruise" patrons and they courteously offered me a lift back to the ship in their taxi. That made me feel good about Vantage.

Then, in the watercolour class, a group of women expressed their enjoyment of the workshop and added: "You should teach on Vantage European River Cruises."

The comment surfaced in my memory more than a year later when the QM2 was being pounded by a hurricane off the north-eastern coast of America. In that situation I asked myself: "What am I doing here?" The thought of calm river water had a definite appeal.

Our first Vantage cruise was on the Russian rivers from Moscow to St Petersburg. Since that first cruise on the *QE2*, I had been running the workshops on my own. But Norene's retirement made the deal even sweeter because she could now come with me.

Watercolour workshops were fitted into the schedule of activities on the Rhine cruise from Amsterdam to Budapest, and cruises on the Black Sea and the Seine and Rhone rivers. The water level might be low or high on a European river, but there are no hurricanes with gigantic waves.

Years later, soon after our final European river cruise, I received a letter from Vantage Deluxe World Travel inquiring if I would be interested in providing 18 watercolours as décor for their next ship. I sent digital photographs of watercolours I had painted during my workshop demonstrations. Vantage selected a collection, and the originals were crated and sent to Amsterdam.

It was an unexpected conclusion to teaching watercolours on cruise ships, and it gave reason to reflect on how art, in its many forms, enriches our lives. We stop to see the sunset, the moon rising over a lake, the vaults of a cathedral, music performances, or to catch the essence of a landscape with quick brushstrokes. The creative process begins with perceptiveness—being aware of the beauty around us and seeing opportunities.

It was a lesson well taught in the pages of Lloyd Rees' sketchbooks. What I did not know in his fine arts class was that there was beginning evidence of a legacy 50 years in the making.

I remembered my first oil painting, one of the six created for the Kiama High School back in 1962. I sometimes wondered what might have happened to the paintings, and on my retirement to Australia in 2006, I drove to Kiama to find out. The school secretary had no idea what I was talking about.

But in 2013, Alan Rees, son of Lloyd, thought he recalled that his father had been "commissioned" in the early 1960s to paint murals for the then-new Kiama High School gymnasium.

A diligent search found the six paintings by the students stacked in an old cupboard—forgotten and damaged from neglect. The Council of Kiama began a restoration project and the alumni office at the University of Sydney provided information on the graduates. Two were deceased.

Four architects—including myself—came together from international practices and retirement to commemorate 50 years on from the Kiama class project. The event was advertised as the Lloyd Rees Legacy project. Alan Rees came from Tasmania and joined us as we stood in front of the six restored paintings, temporarily hung in Kiama's Old Fire Station Gallery. They have since been displayed in a prominent position at the Kiama Public Library.

Louis Pasteur's statement "Chance favours the prepared mind" supports the premise that perceptiveness in seeing opportunities prepares the mind for creativity. If creativity is an endowment from a Being bigger than us, we may see the unexpected—and it may be a pleasant surprise.

---

1 George Molnar, "Swiss Train" in *Molnar at Large: Postcards from Abroad* (Sydney: Angus and Robertson, 1968).

2 Hugh Honour, *The Companion Guide to Venice* (Woodbridge, England: Companion Guides, 1965, Reissued 1996), pages 218, 219.

3

THROUGH MEXICO

While at Ohio State University, I enjoyed many conversations with Professor Perry Borchers on the American Indian cultures of the Southwestern United States. It was part of his interest in all indigenous people, their architecture and art, and ways that their buildings could be recorded.

As Norene and I were planning for a summer trip to the West Coast, it was only natural that I would consult Perry on his knowledge of Southwest Indian textiles and pottery. Norene and I became convinced that an investment in one or the other would be the ideal souvenir of our sojourn in the United States.

We were fortunate to attend the Intertribal Ceremonial in Gallup, New Mexico, during the first week of our 1965 summer vacation. This annual meeting of Native American tribal groups combines music, dance and other art forms in exhibitions and performances. We then visited cliff dwellings and the plains village pueblos, types of North American Indian settlements. The black pottery at the San Ildefonso pueblo, and in particular the work of Maria Martinez, was already famous. She had rediscovered the process of firing pots and platters in low heat ovens to achieve metallic black designs on glossy black surfaces. The pottery was not thrown on a wheel; the clay was coiled and formed by the touch of her hands. We were fascinated by the process and delighted with the results. We were even more excited to meet Maria herself, and her son Popovi Da.

Then we continued on to the West Coast, the Canadian Rockies, and home to Columbus. Our little Chevy Corvair performed admirably for the 16,000-kilometre (10,000-mile) trip and for some months thereafter. Then it began to die.

All too soon, we were nearing the end of our stay in the United States—our exchange visitor visas were for a maximum of two years. As we considered our options for the future, we began to think that an extended visit to the United Kingdom would be a good alternative to an immediate return to Australia. As both the United Kingdom and Australia require driving on the left-hand side of the road, we decided to purchase a right-hand drive Volkswagen directly from Wolfsburg, Germany.

In the meantime, I applied to the University of Edinburgh to continue research towards a doctorate in spatial perception. By continuing research in architecture, I might avoid my Master of Architecture being merely a somewhat esoteric diversion from architectural practice. A few more years of research and a doctorate might lead to an academic appointment—and a new direction for my career.

Our Volkswagen Beetle arrived early in the spring of 1966. The right-hand-drive version was a practical idea in the longer term. In the immediate setting, roadside spectators around the university campus expressed their opinion that it was "very cool." Occasionally, I succumbed to the temptation to add to their interest. I would sit reading a newspaper in the left-hand front seat—where passers-by expected to see the driver—while Norene drove the right-hand-drive vehicle.

Then Dr Don Wilson, a friend from our youthful past in Australia, decided to come to Loma Linda University in California to gain experience with their heart team. To gain an overview of the United States, he signed up for a 90-day–$90 deal that provided unlimited travel across the country on Greyhound buses. We unexpectedly received a message that he could spend a few days with us.

I met Don at the Greyhound terminal, laughed at his Australian accent and brought him home. Somehow, during the evening meal, we talked him into making a visit with us to Kentucky. Our Volkswagen needed a longer drive than just around campus.

Don folded himself into the front seat beside me—the left side. Now it may have been that life lived between seats on buses triggered what happened next. Or perhaps it was that looking out of windows had lost its excitement. Or maybe he was tired and a burst of fresh air was needed. In any event, as soon as we crossed the Ohio River at Cincinnati, Don grabbed his camera and opened the sunroof. Then he stood on the seat taking photographs of the white fences and green fields.

Cars pulled onto the shoulder of the road as we sped along. They did not want to engage a Volkswagen Beetle with half a person they thought to be the driver, standing up through the roof and taking photographs in all directions.

Kentucky's scenery was still on my mind when I returned to teach in the first-year studio at the School of Architecture and Landscape Architecture. This was the setting for me to become acquainted with Pierre, a visiting professor at Ohio State.

Pierre and his wife had left their home in Switzerland for the academic term. One of the assignments given him was to join a colleague and myself every Friday afternoon to grade student work. The design studio met all day on Mondays and Wednesdays and on Friday mornings. At the end of the week, discussing and recording progressive assessments of work from a large class of students could become tedious. On one particular Friday afternoon near the end of term, it was definitely so.

Soon Pierre and his wife would be returning to Switzerland, so my colleague turned to Pierre during a pause in the assessments and said, "Pierre, you should take a break. Why don't you drive down to the green fields and white fences of Kentucky? See some of the Midwest before you leave us."

I quickly joined in on the suggestion, pleased with the memory of Don Wilson's visit and confirming that we would take care of classes during the first part of the following week. Pierre agreed with the plan.

On Monday morning, my colleague and I were ready to meet with students. Then Pierre arrived. "Pierre," we said, "we thought you were taking a break."

He then described how he had arrived home on Friday afternoon and announced to his wife that they would drive across the state line for a short vacation. It would be a pleasant alternative to the usual routine.

They packed a suitcase ready for an early start the next morning. That didn't happen. It was midday when they turned out of their driveway and headed towards the freeway entrance. They had not progressed half a block when Pierre's wife suggested, "Pierre, it's time for lunch. Why would we drive out of town and pass our favourite restaurant, not knowing what we will find down the freeway?"

Pierre swung into the parking area of the restaurant. Almost two hours later, they returned to the car and headed towards the freeway entrance. Within a few blocks, they passed the local cinema and Pierre's wife strained to see the title of the film on the marquee above the line of patrons waiting to enter the matinee performance.

"Pierre! It's the picture we've been waiting to see. What a perfect way to start our vacation!"

Obediently, Pierre turned the car into a parking place. Later, the happy couple came from the cinema and sat in their car. Even before the motor was in drive, Pierre's wife reasoned that it was getting rather late in the day to begin their vacation.

"Pierre, why travel for an hour or so to a motel where the bed will not be as comfortable as our own? Let's sleep in our bed and start the vacation tomorrow."

Pierre drove home and carried the suitcase back into their house. It proved to be the end of a very short vacation.

Heading to Scotland the long way

When Norene and I left Ohio in June, 1966, we took the long route to Scotland. We began by driving our Volkswagen to New Mexico to again visit the Indian pueblos. The San Ildefonso Pueblo was a definite call, and we had saved money for our souvenir of North America. In fact, as we spoke with Popovi Da, we decided to purchase both a jar and a platter—each inscribed with "Maria Popovi 666." The numbers identified the date. We carefully packaged the pottery in a box and posted it to the address of my aunt in England.

The plan was to continue to drive down to the Panama Canal, board a ship for Barcelona, then drive to Edinburgh. Our little tent came in handy once again—sometimes for a night's rest sandwiched in between two busy days and, at other times, a retreat for several days. For Sabbath, we always tried to find a peaceful and attractive campsite. For the first two weekends after crossing the Mexican border, we enjoyed majestic natural settings in national parks.

When Don Wilson visited us in Columbus, he mentioned the work being accomplished by a medical doctor at Montemorelos, Mexico. Don's vision from childhood in Australia was to be a "flying doctor," serving the people of outback Australia. This continuing aspiration was heightened through his interest in the Montemorelos doctor taking medical expertise and supplies to mountainous villages. Our reading of a travelogue for Mexico given to us by the Sanborn Insurance Company clinched our decision to visit Montemorelos. It read:

> Come now to the little city of Montemorelos, Mexico's citrus capital. At left, the famous Seventh-day Adventist Hospital and School—these fine folks are doing a *wonderful* humanitarian job here; excellent hospital; American doctors; nurses training; school for youngsters; printing plant—everything. Visitors are welcome—*do* stop.

We did. And it was an enjoyable visit.

Then we again packed the tent in the car and headed down the highway to Mexico City. On arrival, we parked in a street near the city centre and immediately a large, jovial gentleman seated on a small stool caught our attention. He sat on the sidewalk outside a café and appeared to be the epitome of Mexican hospitality, calling out for us to come and meet him. He soon discovered that we were Australians and that I was an architect with an interest in the Mayan ruins of the Yucatán Peninsula. We thought we were helping him practise English, but there was more to it. He asked us to wait for a few minutes and went inside.

He returned with two books—Volumes 1 and 2 of *Incidents of Travel in the Yucatán*, by John L Stephens. He said he had been waiting for an English-speaking visitor so he could pass them on. I noticed that the original publication date was 1843 and that there were 120 engravings in each volume. We thanked our donor for the gift, and he directed us to the nearby landmarks we had stopped to see.

As we continued our journey to Monte Alban and the base of the Yucatán Peninsula, we found the books fascinating. We read accounts of things like eye surgery to correct turned eyes, and full descriptions of great architecture, with illustrations.

We spent Friday, August 5, at Palenque—finding, sketching and photographing Mayan ruins in the jungle. We left mid-afternoon to drive towards the Pan-American Highway, hoping to find a pleasant campsite somehow carved out of the thick rainforest. But the lack of road signs, ambiguous map information and conflicting directions from people at the roadside, confounded us and led to delays. With sunset hastening, we looked in vain for even a small area where we could pitch our tent.

We started to climb a mountain, and the jungle that until then had created a chasm for the dirt road gave way to rocks. Our map seemed to indicate that we were perhaps 130 kilometres (80 miles) from the nearest town, Tuxla Gutierrez.

We came to a divide in the road, with a new road appearing to lead around the base of the mountain, while the old road climbed steeply. We chose the smoother, easier road, but it ended in a rock pile after a short distance. We stopped the car and spent probably 20 minutes feeling despondent. All we could see were rocks and mountain scenery. There was definitely no campsite. The only prudent thing to do, with darkness closing in, was to go back to the road junction and begin the steep climb.

It was not only steep, but also rocky. The underside of the Volkswagen hit on the rocks, but at least the rough road surface provided friction. We cautiously negotiated the obstacles, travelling at no more than a few kilometres per hour. We turned a corner and, to our surprise, came upon a car parked at the side of the road. It was an even greater surprise when one of a group of Mexicans called out to us.

"Where are *you* going?"

Surprised at the use of English, Norene responded through an open window, "To Tuxla."

"Then you are going right."

I noticed the car had an American licence plate.

"Where are you going?" I ventured.

"We are Seventh-day Adventists. We're going to Linda Vista College just a few miles further on to visit my brother and sister who are students there."

We immediately climbed out of our car, and it took little time to become acquainted. The spokesman for the group was Dr Benjamin Rodriquez, who had recently returned to his family in Montemorelos after a medical internship at the Branson Hospital in Toronto, Canada. He explained that they had gathered by the roadside to pray and open Sabbath, but any further explanation was unnecessary. How happy we were to join them!

Now we could see beyond the conflicting directions, the ambiguous signs and the frustrating delays. Everything had seemed to be against us as we had tried to find a campsite before Sabbath. Even the delay at the rock pile at the end of the new road now made sense. There was a larger plan for a meeting we were meant to attend.

We followed Dr Rodriquez and his family on a side road to Linda Vista. It was so close that the Vespers program was still in progress when we arrived. We sat at the back of the chapel.

"There's my brother in the choir," Dr Benjamin whispered. "That's my sister speaking now."

At the conclusion of the service, we were introduced to these students. But we soon discovered that Mrs Virginia Butler was unable to move her van because of our car, and she was looking for us. She needed to return nurses to the Yerba Buena Hospital. And so we met Dr and Mrs Butler. Despite the inconvenience we had caused, they were pleased to meet us and insisted that we stay in their home.

The next afternoon, on returning from a walk in the surrounding mountains, we found that messengers had just arrived to report an epidemic of cholera in nearby villages. Plans were immediately laid for a team to go and provide medical care. Dr Rodriquez volunteered to stay a week and take part in this work. The incident reminded us of Dr Don Wilson's description of those who brought medical care to mountain villages surrounding the town of Montemorelos.

Several years after our visit to Montemorelos, my brother Keith and his wife Ngaire stopped at the town as they travelled from the port of Acapulco to pick up a Volkswagen campervan in Texas. Perhaps they had come across a copy of the same free insurance booklet we had used as a guide and read the same paragraph. For them, it was a weekend visit, and after the church service, they were invited to the home of a Mexican family.

The host was Dr Benjamin Rodriquez. Hearing Keith's Australian accent, he was anxious to share a personal incident that he said had amazed him. He told how he was driving with a full car of relatives to a college and hospital in southern Mexico, and they stopped right at sunset on a corner of a rough mountain road. Just as they were ready to join hands and offer a prayer to begin Sabbath, a car bounced to a stop and an Australian couple joined them.

We had already shared the story with Keith, but he waited for Dr Rodriquez to finish before announcing that the Australian driver was his brother. Dr Rodriquez responded by commenting about how we are all brothers and sisters. It was some time before Keith's enthusiasm convinced him that this brother was actually his sibling. They both agreed that the precise timing of the roadside prayer was more than a chance meeting.

Norene and I enjoyed meeting Dr Benjamin Rodriquez and his family members from Montemorelos. We also appreciated the hospitality of Dr and Mrs Butler at Linda Vista on our journey through southern Mexico. Before leaving on Sunday morning, we were told of an Adventist clinic just over the Guatemalan border. It was a facility operated by friends of the Butlers, a Dr and Mrs Graves. The Butlers hoped we would visit them, but we expressed hesitation about imposing on the busy lives of church workers. Waving away our concerns, they asked if we would be kind enough to deliver a parcel to the clinic, and would we also leave an order at the pharmaceutical supply centre at Cristobal de las Casas, three-and-a-half hours towards the border?

In Guatemala, we found Mrs Graves at the clinic. She told us that visitors were few and far between, and her husband was away, having been delayed in returning from Washington, DC. We felt the sincerity of her welcome to this oasis of hope in the midst of illness and poverty. And we were given mail to deliver to the Hospital Adventista in Nicaragua.

The roadside meeting with Dr Benjamin Rodriquez and our visit to Linda Vista opened an itinerary for us all the way to the Panama Canal. Along the way, we were inspired by the loyalty of those in mission service. We also knew from personal experience that there are times when Christians can know they are in the right place at the right time.

It would be wonderful to know this all the time, but God ordains that it is not so. The exercise of faith is fundamental to the Christian life amid the turbulence of the world's ocean of events and ideas. Norene and I had no idea that an experience of uncertainty and serious concern lay ahead. That would be in Edinburgh, but for now, the objective was to get there.

Edinburgh and a medical issue

At the port of Panama, we saw our Volkswagen lifted across the bow of a ship that had arrived from the west coast of South America. We moved into a cabin and sailed to the ports of La Guaira, Curaçao and Tenerife. Then we landed at Barcelona, drove to Boulogne and boarded a vehicular ferry to Dover, England.

We were pleased to see the package of Maria Popovi's pottery awaiting our arrival in Dover. Our pleasure was doubled because the contents of our car had been stolen in Costa Rica. As much as we had not wished to lose our slides and books, we were pleased that the parcel of valuable pottery had been in the safe care of the postal service and insurance company.

It was exciting to drive into Edinburgh. I met with my advisors at the departments of architecture and social sciences, and wanting time to clarify my thinking on my proposed research and equipment needs, we drove across the Firth of Forth and camped for another three weeks while we waited for a house in suburban Edinburgh to be vacated.

We soon settled into the routine of our life in Scotland. Norene obtained work as a physiotherapist at a hospital on the road to Glasgow. I travelled by bus to Princes Street and up the hill to the university. Edinburgh is a wonderful city and it provided for all our needs. We were both busy.

One morning, I looked in the mirror and noticed a brown mark on my right eyelid that I had not seen before. Then I recalled that an ophthalmologist in Columbus, Ohio, had commented on a small dot near the eye when I was being tested for a new pair of glasses. I was told to note any change in shape or colour. That I had not done, but I quickly appreciated the alertness of the ophthalmologist.

I visited the student medical office at the University of Edinburgh and soon found myself in the operating theatre at the

Royal Infirmary. After the operation, I returned to my research, but now regularly looked at my eye in the mirror. To my surprise, the mark returned and grew quicker and darker than before.

I paid a return visit to the hospital and was introduced to the leading plastic surgeon in Scotland. He explained the deep incisive procedure he would follow to remove the lesion.

I was not concerned when I awoke in the presence of an array of medical students. After all, this was a teaching hospital and an outstanding surgeon had reason to be proud of a deep "V" incision that would heal perfectly. I thought little more about the incident.

I was busy with research, and my dissertation topic developed. My reading included areas from the disciplines of psychology, physiology and architecture. Through combining ideas and making equipment to record eye movements, experimentation began. The final tome carried the title, "Subjective Responses and Eye Fixations to Visual Displays of Spatial Sequences."

I defended my dissertation in Edinburgh, received word that my application to teach at the University of Newcastle was successful and accepted an invitation to visit Andrews University in Michigan on the way home to Australia.

While there, I presented a lecture on architecture to the student assembly. Then Dr Richard Hammill, the university president, shared with me a vision for an architecture program within the Adventist Church educational system. To him, this meant Andrews University. I was excited by the idea but realised that we were in the area of long-range planning. We agreed to keep in touch.

Norene and I moved into a house in Cooranbong, New South Wales, Australia, and I began to prepare lectures and organise my collection of architecture slides. There was only one negative to the position at the University of Newcastle—I was granted next-to-no medical coverage.

After a year had passed, I visited a local physician as part of an annual medical examination. While there, I asked what might have been written in the report from the Royal Infirmary in Edinburgh, because details on the eye problem had not been shared with me. Apparently, back then this was not unusual. The doctor said he would request a copy of the report.

When it arrived at his office, he summoned me to come in for a briefing.

He was blunt: "It was the worst type of melanoma."

He explained that life expectancy from this kind of melanoma would usually have been not more than six months.

If Norene and I had known this in Edinburgh, I might well have discontinued my research agenda. And it may have led to a different response to Dr Hammill's inquiry of my interest in developing an architecture program at Andrews University.

The experience at the roadside in Mexico provided the knowledge that God was leading us and that we were in the right place at the right time. This knowledge helped see us through other times of uncertainty.

4

AUSTRALIAN ABORIGINAL ART

On my return to Australia, I brought with me a greater interest in Aboriginal art. I had also embraced new skills. At the Ohio State University, I gained expertise in applying the principles of photogrammetry to architecture.

In essence, photogrammetry is the process of taking measurements from a pair of stereoscopic photographs. A visual model of a building is oriented the same way as when the pair of stereoscopic photographs of the building were taken. Looking at the visual model, I could steer a plotting machine to make accurate measurements in three-dimensions. The result was drawings of plans, elevations and sections.

When I joined the Faculty of Architecture at the University of Newcastle, the recording of contour information of complex rock surfaces and Aboriginal art located on them seemed to me to be a good idea. I considered the several areas I would need to address in creating an inventory for research projects. I eyed the Australian Institute of Aboriginal Studies (now the Australian

Institute of Aboriginal and Torres Strait Islander Studies) in Canberra as a potential source of financial grants.

I discovered that the staff at the office of the National Parks and Wildlife Service in Sydney included an enterprising academic poised at the beginning of a successful career in preserving cultural history. Lesley Maynard proved to be a strong supporter of my research interests.

One more element fell into place when I found that the New South Wales Police Department was purchasing equipment that could be used for photogrammetry. Detective Sergeant John Snowden wanted to objectively record the road dimensions and details of fatal traffic accidents by taking stereoscopic photographs on location and then plotting the information on a drawing. He was ardent in his intentions, and his position in department administration provided the budgetary where-with-all for him to purchase a Wild C-120 stereometric camera and an expensive plotting instrument from Switzerland.

These items were precisely what I needed to record Aboriginal art. I also needed someone with a sense of vision and a willingness to share these kinds of "toys." John provided both—and more.

The day I met him and laid out my research agenda, he responded in kind by explaining the nature of his work. Reaching for a jar in which some remains floated in chloroform, John gave me a wry smile and asked if I could tell what the objects were. Unfortunately, I could—they were what was left of a thumb and some fingers.

"Taken from the grille of a hit-and-run '78 Camaro," he said.

I liked John's blend of seriousness of purpose and down-to-earth humour—and his willingness to share, of course.

A researcher needs a research assistant, and the Faculty of Architecture employed a laboratory technician. A bearded, creative man, Peter had developed an attitude of not overdoing it when engaged in setting up lab experiments. My proposal to him was so different to his normal life at work that it appealed. I began our conversation with, "We're going to Mootwingee."

"Where's that?" he replied.

It was the first question of many that needed explanation.

Mootwingee is a site of Aboriginal rock engravings, chiselled into a half-acre of variously tilted rock surfaces—in general on a 23-degree slope. It is located 128 kilometres (80 miles) north of Broken Hill, which in turn is some 1140 kilometres (700 miles) west of Sydney—close to the New South Wales–South Australia border.

The plan was to take some stereoscopic photographs of the rock engravings using the police department's C-120 camera, from a position at least six metres (18 feet) above the Mootwingee site. Lesley Maynard from the National Parks and Wildlife Service recognised the project's validity, for she had written of her concerns about the rapidly deteriorating rock surfaces. High temperatures during the day followed by cold nights cause fracturing of the thin strata. Over time, the outstanding examples of rock engravings would certainly be lost forever if no precise record were made of them. The use of a stereometric model to obtain plan and contour drawings of the site was therefore a piece of valid work.

The only question was how to suspend a scientific camera high above the rock art in a landscape with few vertical elements. Even when there was something tall in the landscape, it might not be where you needed it to be. For this reason, we decided to build a tower, with its feet carefully placed to avoid damage to the engravings. The tower would have a tree-house-like platform, which we could climb up to and take photographs of the site. These photographs would also record steel pins placed in the fissures between the rocks. These targets provided the means for later determining the scale of what we photographed.

The rest of the work could be done in the air-conditioned comfort of Sydney's police department. That's where the Wild A-7 Autograph plotting machine would come into play. It was exactly what we needed.

I approached suppliers of aluminium scaffolding about obtaining materials to build the tower. The oddness of my request

55

appealed to a firm that rented demountable scaffolds, and they offered—for free—as many 20-foot (6-metre) lengths of 4-inch (10-centimetre) tubular aluminium as needed, along with shorter pieces, connecting joints, nuts and bolts.

The idea of using a demountable tower brought with it the challenges of transporting the pieces of scaffolding to a distant and remote site. This is where Peter's ingenuity came in. He knew that the university had teams of fours and eights—muscular men who rowed boats in collegiate competitions. Their record was abysmal, but it did not deter them from visiting other universities.

To facilitate the transport of the rowing boats, the university sports department owned a trailer with bars welded at several heights. In his mind's eye, Peter could see the aluminium tower components transported safely on this trailer.

The use of the trailer was secured, and early one Sunday, Peter and I left civilisation driving the university's Holden station wagon with trailer in tow. The long day began with crossing the Blue Mountains and on to Molong and Nevertire. Nyngan showed as a slightly larger ink blot on our map. We passed small settlements and miniscule railway stations. Mullencudgery had a two-person waiting room. Mandetta's platform was the size of two milk cans. Then we came to the town of Wilcannia.

Miles from nowhere, the town had a small population of scattered families living in humpies near the meagre shade of saltbush shrubs. An old icebox, precedent to the refrigerator, was the only other sign of an address.

Wilcannia's average annual rainfall is 255 mm (about 10 inches)—twice the average of four-fifths of the Australian continent's area. But an average rainfall is only part of the story. Many young children in outback towns have never seen rain until long-awaited downpours suddenly inundate their home with gigantic floods.

We travelled on to a landscape of spinifex and yellow paddy melons. Both were tinted by the red earth. Late in the evening, we drove into the parking lot of the Grand Hotel, Broken Hill. It had been a long day's journey. Peter and I bedded down, happy in the thought that tomorrow—and just a couple of hours' drive—would bring us to Mootwingee. Little did we know!

Our very long outback day

The penny should have dropped the next morning at breakfast. We sat down to a greasy plate of soft eggs and toast. Our lack of enthusiasm for the food led us to listen in on a conversation between two sheep-station owners seated at a nearby table. I was impressed that they had flown their planes to Broken Hill from stations way out somewhere.

They sensed we were listening, so there was a "g'day" and an inquiry as to what we might be doing in Broken Hill.

"We're going to Mootwingee," we replied.

They laughed. Loudly. Then one proceeded to explain that the fords were running north of Broken Hill. He had seen the flooded road crossings yesterday as he flew over the road that led to Mootwingee.

We should have asked for more information, but Peter's determination led him to conclude the conversation.

"Righto! We'd better be on our way," he said.

"Good luck, mate," one of the farmers replied, and they turned back to the day's business.

The breakfast conversation stayed in our minds, but we felt some satisfaction as we counted the miles on the road north. The road was dry and everything seemed to be going smoothly.

"Four miles out of Broken Hill, and it's still tar-sealed."[1]

"Five miles."

So it continued for one or two more miles, then the road turned to gravel. But it was dry gravel. Then red dust.

"Those old farmers sure tried to fool us," I ventured.

"Not a cloud in the sky."

The straight red road was now a single-vehicle width. The station wagon and trailer created a thick cloud of red dust behind us. A slight undulation in the landscape lay ahead, and we slowed for a bend at what seemed to be a dip in the road. It was, indeed, more than a dip. It was a drop—into a creek bed. I braked and we came to a standstill near the edge of the water. It was clear that the ford was usually easily passable but recent rains had swollen the creek.

"So, this is what the farmers were worried about!"

Peter and I reckoned we could deal with it, so we took off our shoes and socks, and rolled up our pants. We waded through the water, which reflected the blue sky, until the mud that swirled up from our feet turned it a dark rusty red. The water was only 30 centimetres (a foot) or so deep. We agreed on the route to take and our plan of action. I would gun the engine of the station wagon and the momentum, with the slight decline on which the trailer was situated, would take us through.

Except it didn't.

Halfway across the ford, the right wheel of the station wagon suddenly sank and the motor stopped. Peter and I opened the doors of the stalled vehicle to the red sea surrounding us. Apparently, in our reconnaissance mission, we had not noticed the loose mud of an underwater hole—left by the hapless incursion of a previous vehicle and the consequent digging of a wheel from the mud.

Nothing would stop Peter now. His methodical laboratory training took over. The wheels of the trailer were still on firm ground, so we detached it from the station wagon. We would use whatever material we could find to drag under the sunken wheel. The theory was that the motor of the vehicle would be so pleased not to have a trailer to pull that, with the encouragement of some traction, it would bring itself to the dry ground on the shore ahead.

The result would be the two vehicles on firm ground, albeit on opposite sides of the flooded ford. This is where we were in our proposed plan when simultaneously our eyes lighted on the aluminium scaffolding tied to the rails of the trailer. It was obvious! We even had the connecting pieces and bolts to create a fixed link between the station wagon and trailer. In our minds, this part of the plan would be easy. The traction of the wheels of the station wagon on the dry road would pull the trailer through.

There were a few scruffy bushes along the creek. These, and whatever else we could find, were gathered ready to place in the muddy water. Then we unhitched the trailer and stuffed the assembled collection of sparse vegetation under the wheel. We started the station wagon and crawled forward. It worked! And it only took half an hour.

Peter and I congratulated ourselves as we stood beside the station wagon on dry land. After a few minutes' rest, we reminded each other that it was still more than 80 kilometres (50 miles) to Mootwingee. We waded back through the water and began to untie some of the scaffolding from the trailer.

That is when we heard a motor vehicle coming from the direction of Broken Hill, and we ran towards the crest. It was a large truck.

The driver, Max, stopped, took in our situation and said, "No sweat, mate! Forget the plan to use the aluminium scaffolding."

Max was big, likeable and easy-going. We could see that he spent most of his time sitting in the cab of the truck, with a case of beer on the passenger seat as his regular companion.

He explained that he would go around the trailer and get through the ford without any trouble. Then he would use his steel cable to pull our trailer across. We would be set, and he could continue his journey to a farmer's homestead a few miles farther on. His mission that day was to load up bales of wool at Farmer Jack's.

We tried to warn Max about the deep hole. But his experience and truck-driving ability more than qualified him to deal with this little flooded creek. He was not about to be advised by two mud-splattered city slickers who had got themselves into a sticky mess.

Peter moved the station wagon out of the way, and I watched as Max took his truck into the water. As he crossed, he seemed to position the front-right wheel close to the hidden hole. Actually, it proved to be the exact location of the hole—and he was stuck.

Max opened the door and stepped down to our level. The immobilised truck was now an obstacle between our station wagon and trailer. But Max, it seemed, was not fazed by dust or red clay, storm or high creeks. We followed his directions, placing the truck jack in the thick murky mess on top of his large spare wheel. Thankfully, the truck was not loaded.

We were all so engaged in the project of getting the truck out of the mud that we did not hear a Land Rover approaching from the opposite direction. Farmer Ted was out on some business trip, and I am sure the parked station wagon heralded trouble to one who knew the road well.

Ted's Land Rover was an older vintage, but it did have a winch and steel rope on the front bull bars. This interested the three of us as we emerged from the water. Ted seemed to be more interested in the refreshments in the cab of Max's truck.

I had heard of the danger of tensioned cables breaking and wrapping around bystanders, so Peter and I watched the rescuing of the truck from a distance. With the cable in place, Ted tightened it on the winch. Max accelerated in the lowest gear. It was slow, but a rather pleasant sight to behold as the truck moved forward. Finally, the truck, Land Rover and station wagon were on the same side of the ford. The trailer now looked lonely across the waterway, but it only took minutes to bring it to us using the cable.

I am not sure if it was the arrival of Ted, or simply the first opportunity for me to stand and reflect, but it came to mind that Lesley, the National Parks and Wildlife Services representative, was flying into Broken Hill from Sydney that morning. She planned to drive a rental car along this same road to be with us and the recording project at Mootwingee.

While she was set for adventure, I thought that her descent into this creek bed was an event she could well avoid. She would speed along the dusty track oblivious of any problem with flooded creeks.

I told the others how Lesley, a Sydneysider, would soon be arriving at the scene. So Max suggested that one of us should go with him to help load the bales of wool at Farmer Jack's station while the other waited for Lesley. I looked at Peter, and he looked at me.

He drew the short straw. After all, he had not met Lesley.

Ted ended up with half the beer as a reward for his labours, and we watched as his Land Rover splashed through the creek bed, avoiding the disaster area. He was happily on his way to his business in Broken Hill.

Then I watched as Max's truck, with Peter in it, headed off in a trail of dust in the opposite direction. I was to pick up Peter at Farmer Jack's after Lesley arrived. I reinforced in my mind Max's instruction to turn left on the road five kilometres (three miles) north towards Mootwingee.

While I waited for Lesley, I connected the trailer and replaced the few lengths of aluminium scaffolding that Peter and I had removed three hours before. This done, I waded through the water, confirming the soundness of the creek bed in a line that would avoid Lesley getting into trouble. Then I sat at the crest of the road in the meagre shade of a saltbush and watched for an approaching line of red dust.

I waited for more than an hour.

Breakfast at the Grand Hotel, such as it was, was ancient history, and I was envious of the meal Lesley would have been served on her flight to Broken Hill. I was not only hungry, I was also incredibly hot. I could feel the sunburn on my face and see it on my arms.

Eventually, a cloud of dust appeared on the horizon. Ten minutes later, a red rental car slowed in response to the waving of my arms. To say that Lesley was surprised to see me standing alone in the desert would be an understatement, but then the day was not a typical one. Even for the outback.

We were glad to see each other. I opened the car door and led her to the brow of the decline. She was amazed to see water, and the murkiness from the past misfortunes had gone, so that the bright blue sky was again reflected on the surface. It belied the struggles of earlier in the day. Lesley thought it was picturesque, with the silhouette of the trailer's rear on the distant rise.

I carefully explained the route for her to take through the ford. Halfway through my explanation, she handed me the car keys. Crossing the ford now proved to be remarkably easy, and Lesley sat next to me enjoying the ride.

After the successful crossing, I drove ahead with an occasional glance in the rear-vision mirror to reassure me that Lesley— shrouded by a cloud of dust—was still following. Thirty minutes later, we drove up to Farmer Jack's homestead. Max's truck stood at the woolshed.

And there was Peter, totally exhausted and with blood on his arms, as the last bale of wool was guided into place on the back of the truck. Peter looked at me. He looked more wild than I had seen him look before. It was good that Lesley was there, giving rise to the need for polite introductions.

Farmer Jack's hospitality came through. Cold refreshments were passed around as we squatted in the shade of the loaded truck. It was now late afternoon. Max had cargo to take to Broken Hill, and he wanted to clear the creek bed before it got too late. And we still had more than half a day's journey left to Mootwingee.

Lesley suggested that she go ahead and prepare a barbecue at the ranger's house at Mootwingee. We had been told that the turnoff was marked by a sign pointing to the right. It was one of those "You can't miss it" claims that solicits extra care.

We watched Lesley leave. Then Peter and I climbed into the station wagon, felt the jerk as the dual wheels of the trailer started to move, and headed down the road. It was remarkably silent. There was nothing we wanted to talk about.

The miles of dust were interrupted by a few minor creek crossings. Peter and I were now adept at the procedure. He would wade through the ford to check the soundness of the bed, and I would accelerate through the water. This continued for a couple of hours. Meanwhile, the bright sky changed to red, then black. In the blackness ahead, we saw a car with its lights facing right.

"It must be Lesley," I ventured. "She's afraid we might miss the turn."

Just then we felt a change in traction, as the road changed from dust to clay.

"Go, Lesley!" I shouted in a useless attempt to get her out of the way. Of course, she wouldn't be able to hear me, but the last thing I wanted to do was to slow down in the mud.

Then our headlights revealed the red rental, broadside in a sea of mud. I tried to detour around the car, following the hand-waving of a lone figure, but the bogey wheels on the trailer jerked us to a sickening stop.

The three of us conferenced, knee-deep in sticky mud.

"No time to waste," suggested Peter. I was relieved to see that the rest after leaving Farmer Jack's station and the presence of Lesley had produced a second wind.

It was determined that this was indeed the turn-off to the Mootwingee site. We would first push and ease Lesley's car to the firm ground close by. This was easy. Then, as we turned towards the more difficult challenge of the station wagon and trailer, a pair of headlights appeared on the horizon from the direction of Broken Hill. We began to make our way towards the lights. To our surprise, the vehicle turned west, apparently on a detour around the bog. Peter and I ran as best we could, waving our arms.

The vehicle slowed and stopped. It was an old Land Rover. To our complete amazement, inside was Ted! Farmer Ted. But he was not the same, having drunk most of the half case of beer.

Ted was alert enough to remember the detour around the acre of mud. He also remembered our encounter earlier in the day. He even knew that we were heading for Mootwingee, and he connected this knowledge with the thought that the two-way radio in the Land Rover cab might be just what was needed. Ted could call the ranger and have him come and tow us out of the bog. We couldn't be far away now, and the ranger would be pleased to know that his friend, Lesley, and her expedition were safe. He could assist in the last hour of the day's journey.

Ted sat in the driver's seat and twiddled the knobs of the radio. Then, holding the microphone to his lips, he began, "Calling Moot-a-wint-gee. Calling Moot...moota...wintgee." Several decades later, the National Parks and Wildlife Service adopted the spelling "Mutawintji" to sound more like the Aboriginal word for the region. Maybe Ted's solicitation was closer to that, but I was sure it would be ignored by the ranger. He sounded more like a drunken swagman than a representative of an east-coast scientific team.

Ted had made the effort. No-one had answered, so it was time to leave. But Peter and I prevailed on his good nature and his great judgment in carrying a steel rope as Land Rover equipment. So, the four-wheel-drive vehicle came around to firmer ground near the station wagon. We hooked up the steel cable, Ted revved his motor and I eased ours. The cable tightened, the mud was reluctant to let go of the trailer wheels, and—the cable broke!

As Ted's Land Rover pulled away from the scene, most of the cable followed.

Two hours later—after eventually extricating ourselves from the mud—Lesley, Peter and I sat around the camp grill at the

Wild C-120 stereometric camera on demountable tower, Mootwingee, north of Broken Hill, New South Wales, in May, 1974.

ranger's station. It was a barbeque to be long remembered. Close to midnight, we walked past the station wagon on the way to bed. It looked like a ruin in the faint light from the generator shed.

The next day, Peter and I assembled the tower at the site of the Aboriginal rock engravings. Just before sunset, with the low angle of sunlight highlighting the artwork, I climbed a 6-metre-long (20-foot) ladder and pulled the tripod and stereometric camera up onto the platform.

Lesley stood behind the structure, away from the engraving site. She expected to stand there for all of the following day. Instead, I pressed the cable release on the camera, then twice more for good measure. I believed the one ASA film on ultra-flat glass plates would fully record the complexity of the site and measured targets.

"It's done," I announced. "Tomorrow we'll dismantle the tower."

Lesley was impressed with both the simplicity and the science of photogrammetry.

Peter and I rested that evening and prepared for our departure the following morning. The ranger offered to fly Lesley back to Broken Hill and return the rental car later in the week. He told us that the flash flood would have receded even by the time we made our return to Broken Hill. The final confirmation of this came at the original ford. We successfully negotiated the now-shallow trickle and stopped on the far side to take a picture.

Then we heard the noise of a plane. It circled. We thought we saw hands waving inside and we waved back. Then it headed off in the direction of Broken Hill.

Going north for the sake of art

The Mootwingee project led to others. My reading and conversations with personnel at the Australian Institute of Aboriginal Studies broadened my knowledge of the geographical areas of Aboriginal art that I could visit. My interest particularly gravitated to Cape York in northern Australia and to the multitude of cave shelters with galleries of paintings there.

I had a fuller appreciation of the artistic quality of the many forms of Aboriginal art, as well as the rich mythology that accompanies these expressions of the art. Body painting, bark painting and cave painting are important windows of history through which the stories of the Aboriginal Dreamings[2] are understood—or at least partly so. This had been impressed upon me during an earlier lecture I attended on Aboriginal bark painting by Jim Davidson.

Jim was a mining engineer living in Melbourne. With an interest in Aboriginal culture, he presented lectures on the spiritual underpinnings of the Dreamings and how these were expressed in art. In the 1960s, he travelled to West Arnhem Land in the Northern Territory and became interested in a particular tribal area where he made several exploratory trips. Before long, he would spend two to three months each year at the tribal site. He would jet into Darwin, take a small plane and local bus to the edge of the Aboriginal community, change from his business suit into old clothes, put the suitcase under a saltbush and walk towards the tribal campfire. He was sensitive to the differences in cultures, so he stopped at a black stump that could be seen on the horizon by the tribespeople. He then slowly moved towards the camp.

Jim was interested in Dreaming stories that had been passed on through generations by word and art. He found the community's bark paintings to be both rich in culture and of high artistic quality. From his long excursions from the engineering office in Melbourne, he received not only insights into tribal stories, but also a valuable collection of bark paintings, which he bartered from the artists. Eventually, he would open an art gallery in Melbourne.

These cultural stories bore a genuine fascination for Jim and his lecture audiences. Yet he knew that they were secret and special to each tribe.

He described an imaginary interaction between a Western academic and an Aboriginal artist. Sitting cross-legged, the artist might chew the end of a piece of bark, dip it into red or white ochre and apply the pigment to the bark—their thoughts on the story being told in paint. The footsteps of an archaeologist or art historian would be an interruption.

"What are you painting?" the professional might inquire, notepaper in hand.

"Ah! This is the mother and here is the pickaninny [child]," the artist replies, hoping a little information will suffice. It doesn't. So a story develops whereby the boy was disobedient, swam in the water of the lagoon and was attacked by leeches. The notetaker records all the details. This version of the story will later be compared with others and provide material for scholarly articles and conference papers.

Jim knew that for all the off-the-cuff versions, there was one inside story—one that the Aboriginal community would keep in secret to pass on to the next generation.

During the several months each year that Jim spent living with the Aboriginal tribe, he heard more and more of the mythologies. And he came to understand that details were revealed only late at night sitting around the campfire.

After 12 years, Jim was made half-brother to the tribe. There was now an understanding that the old men of the tribe would slowly share with Jim the most closely held secrets of their culture. The young men were leaving the campfire to live a hybrid existence at the edge of civilisation. Life was lived under the shade of a stand of bushes in between excursions to a work location or the distant post office to collect a government cheque. Sadly, too often, it was then off to the pub.

The old men of the tribe came to see Jim as a caretaker of tribal lore. It was somehow understood that he would not share the knowledge he was receiving until the last tribal elder died. Along with his other qualities, Jim was patient.

In the 14th year, he was again at the campfire. The conversation turned to the opossum tree story. He had gleaned much of this particular inside story, but there was a gap until that evening. The revelation of a final piece of information led him to exclaim, "That was important to know. Why didn't you tell me that before?"

A tribal brother smiled and replied, "You come back next year, and we'll tell you some more."

Jim's lecture and my increasing association with professionals at the Australian Institute of Aboriginal Studies in Canberra led me to adopt a healthy questioning of treatises on mythology and a greater recognition of the value of objectively recording Aboriginal art. Photogrammetry was providing the means for this.

My friendship with Detective Sergeant John Snowden at the Sydney Police Department continued. John now had a small team of colleagues who could plot the site of a collision and the tyre marks on the road using the Wild A-7 Autograph. John had also acquired a new item of camera equipment that was ideally suited to the stereoscopic recording of Aboriginal cave paintings and engravings at the scale and diversity existing in Cape York.

Details for a research project there came into focus. The Australian Institute of Aboriginal Studies selected the location— the recently named Early Man Shelter, north-west of Cairns. A group of internationally respected archaeologists, anthropologists and prehistorians from London, Paris, and North America would form a team and conduct an archaeological dig, while I recorded the engravings located on the wall of the shelter.

Many sites of Aboriginal art were being discovered in the bush country of Cape York. Certain topographic conditions seemed to indicate where these sites might exist. One important factor was the presence of spring water.

On the first evening at our destination, the group sat around a fire on a large rock outcrop just below Early Man Shelter, near a spring. In addition to the company of overseas visitors, First Australians were represented in our group—an Aboriginal tracker was a member of the team. Aboriginal people had drifted to the shores of north Australia in smaller craft than the European convict ships of the so-called first settlers, and they did so thousands of years before. Interestingly, a man of Irish convict descent was also a member of the team. These two members of our party helped put our expedition into a larger perspective.

The previous day we had travelled by road from Cairns to Laura, a town consisting of a corrugated-iron hotel, a petrol pump and a generator shed. That night, at the Laura Hotel, the air remained hot and the windows to the few hotel rooms were kept open. After the hotel's greasy breakfast, we set out in three Land Rovers following rough roads, then cross-country. The final few kilometres were on foot, and we shared in carrying the gear.

Conversation abruptly changed that evening when one of our group saw the outlines of engravings on the rock where we sat. The fire's fluctuating flames lit the depressions obliquely. We were prepared for the engravings at the Early Man Shelter, but these engravings at the campsite near the spring were a surprise. It was then clear to us that the spring of water had provided continuity between our camp and a campsite thousands of years old.

Our work began the next day. The group assembled in the Early Man Shelter hoping to learn something of the thoughts of those who had first inhabited the place. A battery-operated light was put in place in the late afternoon, and I taped some measured marks onto the rock surface and positioned the tripod holding the stereometric camera. A long exposure recorded the art and information on the nature of the surface. The camera was moved three times, and my work was done.

I was fresh and clean at the end of the day. Not so the archaeologists. They had lightly brushed the black floor all day, looking for arrowheads and food remains, and were covered in dirt. Perhaps they saw that as evidence of their day's work— certainly a contrast to a photographic science.

With my work complete, I was commissioned to assist in the excavation on Day 3. That day of digging and brushing the black earth was enough. I was alert for change as we sat around the campfire after supper. When the conversation turned to the colours and forms of Aboriginal rock painting, I seized the opportunity.

"Tell me more about Percy," I ventured.

Following Percy's lead

I had pieced together that a man called Percy Trezise held valuable information on the locations of rock galleries. The following description is from his book, *Rock Art of South-East Cape York*:

> My occupation as an airline and aerial ambulance pilot took me daily on trips across the length and breadth of Cape York, and I was able to study the geology and topography of the country to determine those areas which offered the best prospects of containing rock shelters suitable for habitation—and consequently, for paintings.
>
> Concentrating on the sandstone areas, I fly as low as possible whenever weather conditions permit and map the most likely looking sites to contain shelters with a north or westerly aspect and adjacent to a possible permanent water supply. In some of the more open shelters, it is possible to see the actual paintings in the brief glimpse afforded as the aircraft flashes past. The aerial surveys are followed up by driving as near as possible by Land Rover and then carrying the swag for upwards of a week, to investigate the area thoroughly on foot.[3]

Percy's ability to know which part of the bush he had just seen and to mark it on the map, while flying across the very large Cape York Peninsula, was impressive. Even more staggering was Percy's follow-through to find the rock outcrop. Sometimes it was a false alarm. At other times, the result was an art gallery of giant horses, emus, humans, spirits, snakes and koalas.

Percy would then assemble a frame with strings to form a grid. Placing the frame against the rock surface, or wherever it suited the undulations or curves, he would draw the animal and human shapes onto graph paper.

The rock paintings appealed to me on every level. I found the colourful images more interesting than the short shallow cuts in the monochrome rock surface of the Early Man Shelter, and the complex, undulating surfaces sounded like a challenging—but enjoyable—opportunity for science.

In response to my question, the group leader said, "Five miles (8 kilometres) or so from here, Percy found an art site under a large overhanging rock. He called the impressive paintings Possum Gallery. You want a challenge? Try Possum!"

So plans were made for the following day. Our tracker would guide me to Possum Gallery. He would carry the tripod and I would take the camera. He would return to base camp by nightfall, and I would do my work the next day. The plan was for him to return at the end of the day.

I have never taken note of the lay of the land as carefully as I did on the outward journey—just in case something happened to prevent or delay the tracker's return. I could not fail to notice the soft colours of the sandstone outcrops punctuating the stands of eucalypts. We followed ridges and with what seemed only one or two minor corrections the guide brought me to Possum Gallery.

He put the tripod near the deepest overhang, smiled, and said, "OK, mate! Give it a burl!"

I watched him disappear back into the bush, then I placed the stereometric camera next to the tripod and looked around.

Possum Gallery had a large interior space. A wide overhang on the northern side continued on the east and west sides. Several groups of painted figures were on the ceiling and overhangs. The gallery was the focal point of an incredible array of rock outcrops. It seemed that severe erosion had gouged avenues from a plateau. Now, rounded rocks twice my height towered above me. Occasionally, a tree would punctuate the sequence of spaces.

I walked through the area, becoming more and more thoughtful of the place once being home to an Aboriginal tribe. I could imagine women and children sitting high on the rocks. Along the avenues were impressive examples of rock paintings. I stopped for several minutes to admire an incredibly beautiful painting on the rock wall. It was of a hunter—a metre (3 feet) tall—with a bush turkey in one hand and a fish in the other.

I was lost in the past. The significance of Possum Gallery as a cultural centre was obvious. I retraced my steps towards it, experiencing a new corridor on the way. It was amazing to think that Percy and I were two of a very few Westerners to have seen this place.

My thoughts were still with the past Aboriginal settlement when I was almost run down by a wild pig racing out from under Possum Gallery rock. I had arrived back at the pile of my gear. In my absence, the pig had come to investigate the scene and my return caused a mutual surprise.

My earlier plan to sleep inside the confines of Possum Gallery was revised. Instead, I selected a high position on a nearby outcrop. That night, the Southern Cross and a myriad of stars provided my canopy.

The day spent alone at Possum Gallery was one of my best. Among the gallery of animals, I had recorded the form of an 8-metre-long (24-feet-long) snake painted on the vertical and overhanging surfaces of the rock. The photographic glass plates would be filled with animals, including an echidna and possums. A koala was tucked into a curve of the snake in a rock depression.

All these memories came back forcefully three months later, as I sat in a restaurant outside the village of Heerbrugg, Switzerland.

Author's sketch of Aboriginal rock paintings and meeting a wild pig at Possum Gallery, Cape York Peninsula, August, 1974.

Detective Sergeant John had plenty of work for the police department's A-7 plotter, and he had no idea how one could plot contours and artwork from various inclined camera axes. Neither did I. The idea of tilting a stereometric camera at angles between 30 degrees and 60 degrees was not the textbook method for terrestrial photogrammetry.

The head office for Wild equipment at the border of Switzerland and Austria supported the possibility for me to complete the photogrammetric recording of the research project, in the cause of science and art. After several days in Heerbrugg, and with a beginning measure of success, my host invited me to dinner at a mountaintop restaurant. He drove up the hillside and we walked 2 kilometres (1.2 miles) to a dining room thrust towards the valley. It was an experience of great food served in a room with a dramatic view. Swiss people know how to live.

The sophistication of this dining experience on a rock outcrop brought back the contrasting memories of Mootwingee's dust and swollen creeks, and the basics of life on Cape York. In the delightful human setting of the restaurant that evening, I reflected on how the artistic value of Australian Aboriginal art had added to

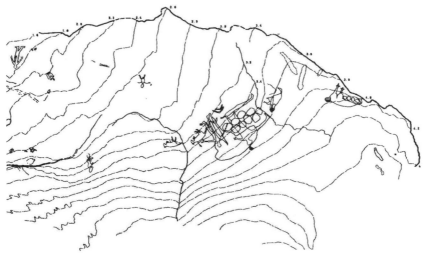

Photogrammetric plotting on section of Emu Gallery, performed by the author at Wild Heerbrugg, Switzerland.

the compass of my life. My mind revisited the beautiful painting near Possum Gallery—the high artistic quality of the hunter holding his wild turkey and fish.

My graduate studies had made it possible for me to combine the understanding and application of photogrammetry with a new appreciation of Dreamtime mythology and its expressions in art.

Unfortunately, the history of English settlers was unkind to Australia's first people. Even church organisations insisted on the separation of children from parents so that the next generation could be "educated." It was not until 2008 that the Australian parliament voted an apology for this "stolen generation."

I walked back along the path that followed the ridge, fully satisfied with a wonderful dinner and appreciative of the journey that had brought me there.

---

1 This was before the metric system came into use in Australia.

2 For a description of this, see Peter Sutton (Editor), *Dreamings: The Art of Aboriginal Australia* (New York: The Asia Society Gallery, 1988). For up-to-date information about what the Dreaming means to First Nations peoples, see <https://www. shareourpride.org.au/sections/our-culture/index.html>.

3 P J Trezise, *Rock Art of South-East Cape York* (Canberra: Australian Institute of Aboriginal Studies, 1971), page 7.

5

AFRICA

I was in the formal lounge of a rich man's home in an African capital city. Seated next to me was a doctor from overseas. The vice-chancellor of a nearby university, along with three other visitors, made up our team of six. On the other side of the doctor was an empty chair. By its location and elaborate design, I knew that this was where the gentleman we were visiting would sit.

The rich man entered the room and went directly to his chair. Before venturing into the reasons for our visit, my doctor friend reached into his briefcase and produced a health product. He named it and indicated how it would benefit the rich man's health. He passed the product to the host who smiled and said, "Thank you."

My doctor friend reached into his briefcase again, produced another item, extolled its virtues and passed it to the host. He smiled again and said, "Thank you."

This ceremony was repeated several more times. When the last health item was in the hands of the rich man, he smiled and said, "Thank you. But why are you here?"

Then came the surprise—for me. The doctor said, "My friend, Dr Clouten, will tell you why we are here."

I had to think fast. I wanted the solicitation to be successful. But I wondered how I could make a request for a donation worth millions without having had the opportunity to research the life and interests of a potential donor. All I knew was that this gentleman owned a bank and made money in business.

"It is a pleasure to be in your country," I began. "We are staying at a church-owned university in the city. . . Have you heard of it?"

"Yes," he replied, "but I have not visited it."

I continued my speech, mentioning that the university had a good nursing program and new science laboratories. I closed with a request: "The university needs a medical school. Would you be interested in donating funds for this medical school?"

"Yes," he replied.

The vice-chancellor almost fell out of his chair.

"But there is something else," our potential donor continued. "I want to do something for my people—a hospital in the minority region of the country's population."

The rich man accepted an invitation from the vice-chancellor to attend a university board meeting to discuss the funding, and I received a report of what took place. Unfortunately, the negotiations broke down when some of the board members offended the donor with their questions about the amount of funding he would supply and their reluctance to support a hospital in the minority region of the country. The medical school remained a dream.

Uganda

It was not my first excursion into Africa. I had visited the continent several years earlier with the same doctor who had called on me to give the impromptu solicitation.

I first met Dr Samuel DeShay in Edinburgh and came to know him well as we walked across the Scottish moors on weekends. He had worked in the war-torn area of Biafra, Nigeria, as director of a hospital until the civil war forced him to leave in 1967. The thought of gaining a fellowship in the Royal College of Surgeons in Edinburgh crossed his mind as a useful addition to his medical credentials, but on his arrival in Scotland, the needs of Africa took precedence, and he began to write a book on nutrition for

Africans. Sam's wife, Bernice, was a nurse. Edinburgh provided a place for her to add a certificate in midwifery to her qualifications.

Sam was a medical practitioner, minister and musician—a pianist and composer. His qualifications, dedication and love for Africa and its people were exceptional. As we walked in the Scottish landscape, Sam painted vivid word pictures of Africa's needs and shared visions of meeting enormous health challenges. I responded with some architectural thoughts on his ideas.

As fellow visionaries, we quickly came to appreciate each other. However, the experiences Sam encountered while working in Africa provided a dose of practicality to keep his feet firmly on the ground even while his head was in the clouds.

I had not experienced the countries of eastern Africa. That changed, thanks to Sam and another medical practitioner, the first Ugandan national to gain membership in the British Medical Association: Dr Samson Kisekka.

Samson was a born leader. His plans to begin his professional life in Uganda as a physician were revised when he attended an evangelistic tent meeting in Kampala. His new horizon was to pursue a medical internship at an Adventist hospital in the United States, and that is where he met the African American Sam DeShay, who had just graduated from Loma Linda University Medical School. That was in 1956. The two interns became lifelong friends.

Both doctors worked in Africa—Samson in Uganda and Sam in Nigeria and several other African countries.

Samson was in trouble in his own country. General Milton Obote and Idi Amin changed the beautiful place that Winston Churchill referred to as "the pearl of Africa" into a dictatorship of terror. Samson's home and farm were destroyed, and he went into hiding knowing he was one of the "intelligentsia" on the death list. A few friends helped him to escape to Kenya on Christmas Day, 1981. In Nairobi, he taught weekly Sabbath school classes while being leader of the Uganda National Resistance Movement. His story is told in Delbert Baker's *From Exile to Prime Minister*.[1]

On January 29, 1986, Yoweri Museveni led an army coup and took control of Kampala. He immediately contacted Samson in Nairobi and invited him to return to Uganda as the country's prime minister. He agreed.

Three years later, at Samson's request, I went to Uganda with Dr Samuel DeShay and a team to visit several of the 84 islands off the western shore of Lake Victoria. These were the Ssese Islands— the term "ssese" means "isolated." The team's objective was to consider ways that the largely unknown and sparsely inhabited islands could be integrated into a comprehensive development involving fishing and agriculture, education, health and tourism. In doing this, the Ssese Islands might provide a model for the rest of Uganda and help jump-start the economy.

That was not to be—at least not in the optimistic time-frame that was envisioned. However, the process of planning provided benefits in many ways.

As the team met in Kampala, Sam and Prime Minister Samson alternated in injecting ideas into our group discussions. We considered the implications of different strategies and began to plan a program for land allocation on a dozen islands. We created designations such as an island for cultural expression, a children's land of play, which we termed *terrain de jeux*, an island to celebrate life extension, a mediation conference centre and an island venue for sharing the best of the continent of Africa.

We created diagrams of organisational structures both for a not-for-profit and a for-profit corporation. For the latter, President Yoweri Museveni was patron and Prime Minister Samson Kisseka the corporation president. At one level of planning, the financial plan and applications for seed money took precedence; at another, the philosophical underpinning of the worth of the individual and a gentle, ecologically responsive architecture was paramount.

Even though he was prime minister, Samson was with us the whole time—on the small ship and in the Land Rovers that had been planted on remote island locations. We slept on floor mats at night in the ruins of a building. More accurately, we rested there and sometimes slept, while soldiers talked outside the open window. They provided a symbolic presence and were ready just in case we were in danger.

While on the ship, the prime minister's chef prepared meals of fish and potatoes. It was during such a meal that I watched for an hour as an African American and a Ugandan national stood close together in the bow of the ship, sharing their past lives and hopes for the future of Africa. It was great to see the meeting of two minds—it was symbolic of the larger venture.

The Ugandan national was Israel Mayengo, a corporation leader in Kampala and one of the five members of parliament who joined the Ssese Islands operations team. Israel and I became good friends during this expedition. One day, he shared his dream for a home and lodge for 25 guests on the island of Bukasa.

On several occasions, Samson invited me to discuss the development of his small hospital in Kampala. He envisioned its extension to a 100-bed facility with two operating theatres. It would become the hospital for the Kisekka Foundation.

The dream of developing the Ssese Islands into a "City of Hope" continued across several visits to Uganda with Dr Sam DeShay. Plans for income-producing projects began with agriculture and led to meetings with Bugema School—now a university. It was envisioned that academic programs in business and education could develop from the agriculture base. Architectural agendas were shared with the faculty of the fledging Department of Architecture at Makerere University. And Sam's ultimate vision for a School for Preventative Medicine was never forgotten.

The not-for-profit Pan-African Development Corporation hosted an international student competition for low-cost housing in Africa. Prizes were awarded to students at MIT, the University of Florence and UC Berkeley.

During that time I was dean of the College of Architecture and Design at Lawrence Technological University in Michigan, and I saw the opportunity for that institution to enter the picture. On my third visit to Uganda, in 1998, I carried with me seven large boards prepared by a junior-level architecture student. The design project was for an African Cultural Centre complex, and the student, Rebecca Bertolini, had summarised the proposal on the first board:

> The African Cultural Centre project is an attempt to preserve the heritage of the African continent. An African American museum and African continental museum, a conservatory, library and language institute form a series of cascading, modern buildings from the top of a hill to the shore of Lake Victoria. History and culture would be preserved, studied and advanced in a setting utilising the latest technologies.
>
> A Hall of Excellence would bring all the countries of Africa together under one single pyramidal structure. It would be a light obelisk, the top of the pyramid illuminated to provide a nightly landmark seen across Lake Victoria. Utilising the latest audio-visual and interactive technologies, the Hall would display and preserve past culture and heritage. Visitors would sense the forces propelling the vast continent into the 21st century.

The idea and the graphic representation raised eyebrows in a positive way as soon as the boards were lined up in the VIP lounge at the Entebbe airport, Uganda. Then they were exhibited in Kampala and later in 1998 in Washington, DC.

I invited the Professor of Urban Planning at Lawrence Tech to join the team and visit the Ssese Islands. He was excited by the project and its educational value to architectural students. Senior students progressed through an impressive learning experience to design a new town for a culture vastly different to that of North America and a climate different to Michigan.

The students produced a book, and 200 presentation boards and 27 models were illustrated in it. All originals were packed in a rental truck and driven to Washington, DC. There student representatives set up an exhibition fit for a president. It was timed to coincide with an official visit by President Yoweri Museveni to the United States.

During my next visit to Uganda, I remember travelling with Dr Samson Kisekka in the back seat of the official Mercedes. The visiting team and Ugandan nationals had met in Kampala for a few days to discuss the details for this visit to the Ssese Islands. The cars for transportation were readied, a boat to go from Entebbe to the islands was arranged and gasoline delivered to the wharf. We were to leave early the next morning.

No-one had thought of arranging a mid-morning breakfast en route from Kampala to Entebbe. So, as we passed through a village, the lead car stopped outside a restaurant and the spokesman went inside to alert the owner that Prime Minister Samson Kisekka had come for breakfast.

A bewildered restaurant owner saw the group of dignitaries assembling outside. What could he do, for he had no food! He wanted to run to the neighbours and ask each for a few eggs. But he knew it was a lost cause. Disappointed, he saw the cars leave. I imagine he still recalls to his children and grandchildren the story of the time he almost entertained the country's beloved prime minister.

In 1999, a delegation of Ugandan dignitaries visited Southfield, Michigan, and attended a ceremony on Lawrence Technological University's home turf to commemorate and celebrate Southfield and Ssese becoming sister cities. This enhanced understanding, and friendship fostered cultural and commercial ties. The many events proved to be a dress rehearsal for the finale at the United Nations headquarters in New York City, where the Lawrence Tech students were invited to display their presentation materials, previously exhibited in Kampala, Southfield and Washington, DC.

Our exhibition was held in a meeting room at the top of the United Nations building. Then we lunched with Dr Samson Kisekka and his wife, the guests of honour. It was the culmination of a valuable learning experience for the architectural students.

I received many letters from those who came with me to the United Nations, and it was evident that the long hours in research analysis and studio design were worth every minute. Expressions of appreciation were also received from international delegates, including Samson and his wife, and for the students these were treasures for a lifetime.

While most of the members of the original team for the Ssese Islands development have now passed away, including Sam DeShay, his dream has continued with some successes and many setbacks. It has not dimmed the vision for medical and humanitarian service to the continent of Africa.

Samson Kisekka has been memorialised in the building of a small clinic at Kalangala on the Ssese island of Bugala. I would like to see a significant piece of architecture built to commemorate his life of Christian service and the continuing work of the Kisekka Foundation. But, like the man himself, the simple, humble structure serves those in need, and speaks volumes in doing so.

I often think of the time I visited the home of Israel Mayengo during its construction on the island of Bukasa. The combination of local materials and imported technology were being brought together in a new way. I admired the creativity and craftsmanship guided by the mind and hands of Israel.

One day he said to me, "Let me take you to my chapel."

We zigzagged along the narrow path to the water's edge and turned left onto a small promontory that jutted out into the water. There, a carefully selected fusion of two small tree trunks had been stuck in the moist ground. The form was that of a cross. It was where Israel Mayengo meditated as the first rays of sunlight gave definition to the soft waves that lapped the shore of Lake Victoria.

This was a chapel experience that helped put the Uganda agenda in perspective.

Nigeria

The excursions to Uganda's Ssese Islands and the meeting with the rich man in his home in a capital city might have been the end of my visits to Africa. But in 2005, Sam DeShay telephoned me and suggested that I pack my bags for a trip to Nigeria.

Back when he was working at the hospital in Biafra, Sam visited Lagos and the home of Chief Michael Ibru.

Chief Ibru was well known in Lagos. When British companies placed high charges on the use of wharves in Nigeria, the chief built new wharves and ships. The "Fish Man" became very rich, with 80 corporations to his name, including an airline and a bank.

Some 30 years after Sam first met him, Chief Ibru experienced a deterioration in health. It was indirectly reported to Sam that the idea of a hospital project might be revisited. So we came to Nigeria.

Nigerians are streetwise entrepreneurs. In Lagos or the Niger Delta—or wherever oil flows—some Nigerians take the initiative to drill small holes in the transportation pipes and fill jerry cans for retail sale. It is one way to avoid the middleman. Unfortunately, lives are often lost in attempts to siphon some of the profits out of the pockets of the very fat companies.

The cover story of the May 22, 2006 issue of *Time* magazine (Europe, Middle East and Africa version) read:

> Last week, more than 150 people died when an oil pipeline on the outskirts of Nigeria's biggest city, Lagos, west of the Delta, exploded in a massive fireball. . . . The pipeline, which ran under a beach, had been uncovered. Small holes had been drilled in it through which thieves could tap off fuel. The leaking pipeline had attracted local villagers who were filling containers when it blew. Nigeria's Red Cross said that the explosion ignited hundreds of gallons of fuel.[2]

I saw an explosion ready to happen on my first visit to Nigeria. A truck was on its side and traffic crawled past the underside of the chassis. It was not until we were level with the vehicle that I saw gasoline draining from the truck. It was a petrol tanker. I was anxious and every metre we travelled away from the truck took too long. Eventually, I could breathe normally again.

The driver of our car simply stated: "We'll go back by a different road. There will be an explosion that closes this road."

Unfortunately, the dream for a Chief Michael Ibru Hospital also exploded. The chief's family had other ideas on how to spend their fortune.

My several excursions into Africa had one thing in common. They were connected to the field of architecture and hospital development. They were large project proposals and—except for some minor achievements—the dreams did not see the light of day.

Several years later, an opportunity came to me from an individual in Africa who reached out to get my attention. I was not seeking a project and almost missed becoming involved.

Kenya—and finding Faith

A complex situation began very simply. Dr Humberto Rasi was the editor of *Dialogue*—an international journal that aimed to connect with young people studying in universities around the world. It was a quarterly journal, published in four languages, and the articles were broadly about science and theology.

To create a balance, Dr Rasi decided to include an interview with an artist in one of the issues each year. I was interviewed for the Spring, 2005 edition, and a colour portfolio of my watercolours was included.

When the interview was published, Dr Rasi thought it would be a good idea if my email address was included—someone might be interested in purchasing a watercolour. That did not happen. However, I did receive about 100 requests for financial help. The common denominator was a need for education.

Not knowing which email requests were genuine, I proceeded to delete them all. With a few, I hesitated, wanting to believe that the story presented was a sincere request.

Four years later, in June, 2009, I received an email which claimed to be from a girl in Kenya:

> Greetings in the Lord's name.
> I am called Faith Akoth. I am a Seventh-day Adventist young girl aged 12 years and an orphan. My parents

died of AIDS in the year 2005. I am a member of Pathfinder class and children's choir....I know you might be wondering how I came to know you. Just know that I was referred to you by God.

I need to be your friend. I need you to accept me as part of your family, to let me be your daughter if it can be possible, for I don't have a parent or anyone to care for me.... Since my parents died, I have never gone back to school. I need an education. Please help me.

Your friend

Faith

I could not easily delete this email. Yet, I considered that perhaps the writer was a third-party scammer, who knew enough about the Adventist Church to create a plausible plea for money.

Norene and I decided to respond, but we would ask questions for verification that might discourage anyone other than a 12-year-old orphan with genuine zeal. We composed an email that requested the names, telephone numbers and email addresses of the church pastor, Pathfinder leader and choir director.

Answers to some of our questions came without delay, but the writer recommended that we contact an Aunt Lilly, who wore the title "Aunt" but was not a relative. We emailed Lilly Ouma and asked for particulars. Her response provided a lengthy explanation.

She described Faith as a bright 12-year-old girl with a burning desire to go back to school. Both parents had died within a month of each other in 2005. Lilly indicated that she had found Faith, who now lived with her in the village of Rapogi, within the Luo culture of western Kenya. It soon became clear that Lilly and Faith were communicating as one.

In our early interactions, there were times when we had a natural tendency towards scepticism, and we questioned the reality of a genuine connection with the village of Rapogi. We also worried about security. However, my attempts to be sensitive to people and situations of another culture were reciprocated by Lilly's respect for keeping our correspondence private. We received only one email gained by theft of our information. It reported that Faith had left her laptop in the back of a taxi and needed money urgently. Riding in a taxi with a computer was not the way things happened in Faith's world, and so we were not deceived by the email.

As our correspondence continued, we heard of both exciting times and some difficult times. When Lilly had malaria, Faith carried her bag as they walked to the hospital. Later, it was Faith's turn and her bout with malaria was severe. Lilly brought food to her and slept under Faith's hospital bed.

Norene and I decided to help. Lilly provided information on the availability of schools, recognising that it was now midway through the 2009 school year. St Theresa Catholic School provided the highest available academic standard. There were limited places, and the tuition was beyond the reach of most families. There was also mention of the local public school, over-populated with more than 100 children to a classroom.

I inquired if there was a library in the town for Faith and paid a monthly library fee to the St Theresa School. Faith immediately followed through with daily visits to the library and wrote that she loved the library and was reading a lot of books. Further evidence of her excitement for learning came in an email written in response to one we had sent to her while I was teaching watercolour workshops on a European river cruise. I had mentioned the city of Vienna. She commented that she had found Vienna in an atlas and that the city was in Austria where German was the spoken language. She asked if we spoke German.

There was an internet café of sorts in the village of Rapogi, sometimes without power and often without internet connections. When operational, it provided the opportunity for email contact— and we hoped that this was with Faith and Lilly. Within a year of our initial contact the "internet café" closed.

The next year, we arranged for Faith to join a boarding school several hours and three bus journeys away. She showed incredible dedication to learning and worked hard to catch up on the four years she had been out of school. Email correspondence with Faith was infrequent but we looked forward to these communications. Her dedication to the church, her sensitivity and concern for the needs of others were impressive for a young girl. In turn, we tried to be sensitive to her culture—Kenya's Luo minority—of which we knew little. Our thinking expanded a familiar axiom to "Think and act globally and locally—with sensitivity and care."

Faith wrote the following from Rapogi during a term break:

> How are you, Mama and Baba? I pray for you every day. Tomorrow we will be in church the whole day. I will be singing with the children. I taught them a new song from the camp-meeting. Then we also have songs to sing in our small group and in the Pathfinders. So, I have a lot to prepare and be ready for tomorrow.

> Below is a poem I wrote to you last night and dedicated to you. My humble request is can someone read you the poem and as you listen you can assume it is me telling you the words.

Here are a few sentences from the poem:

> After my first mama and baba left me, I knew it was the end of all. I cried and argued with my God and told him all my pain and grief. I told him I was lonely.

> Today I am blessed and am happy. I am no longer lonely or in pain. I am so happy because I have a mama and baba who care for me. I will continue praising my God for answering my prayer as long as I live.

Norene and I travelled to Egypt in December, 2010, and we visited Kenya a week prior to our cruise on the Nile.

What a joy to visit with Faith and Lilly! We arrived at the Ouma family home in the village of Rapogi late in the afternoon. The buildings were located around a courtyard according to strict planning principles. In keeping with the Luo traditions, Lilly's father has five wives, and each has a house. The first wife's house is directly opposite the entrance to the courtyard. Lilly's mother is wife number three, and her home is to the right of the first wife's house.

As soon as we arrived, we were greeted and taken to comfortable chairs interspersed with low tables. This was the first of many experiences that made us feel welcome. All the family and the community also wanted to greet us. On many occasions, the room was filled with adults and children. There were about 12 small children in the Ouma family, and the home was shared with almost as many orphans of no relation.

Lilly had organised two community meetings for one afternoon. While Norene met with the women, I joined the men in the shade of beautiful trees and trellises. I asked what the men would like to discuss. The response was immediate: "We have a dream for a primary school. There are many orphans."

The men were convinced that we had come to Rapogi Lwanda to help them build a school. We did not know that Lilly had already gone to Nairobi to register a Rapogi Lwanda self-help community-based organisation with the government office. She had also started to teach the local children using a blackboard and chalk in the shade of a large tree.

To the community, the story of Faith was peripheral. They believed that our visit to their village and the meeting at 3 pm on December 27, 2010 were evidence that their dream to build a primary school had begun to be realised.

Norene and I were convinced otherwise. We could assist Faith in her education, and she would be a leader to her community and culture. Our association with Rapogi was about Faith. Nothing more.

That changed on our return to Australia. The idea that we might be involved in an African school project came to the fore through unrelated circumstances. We had purchased a villa in Queensland while living in North America. To hold this for our retirement years in Australia, we had rented the waterfront villa on long-term leases. Our return from Africa in January, 2011, coincided with the need to find a new tenant. Until then it had been easy, but the usual notice for tenants on the waterfront failed to raise any inquiries.

We visited the real estate office only to be told there was little hope for new tenants. By the beginning of March, we were getting concerned because our travel plans took us overseas in early April. The villa had been an asset, but without a tenant it would quickly become a liability.

We knew what our friends in Kenya would do—pray and believe. We made the rental a matter of prayer and asked for a tenant by March 31. We added the promise that if that happened, we would provide the funds for the first classroom at Rapogi Lwanda.

The only inquiry to the real estate office was on March 30 and a long-term lease was signed the following day. This might have been a coincidence. We chose to believe it was something more.

We shared the story with my brother Keith, who at the time was assisting in setting up a library in Nairobi. He responded, "If you provide the first classroom, we will donate the second."

Then there was more. Keith said, "I will go to Rapogi and scope out the project for the organisation A Better World Canada." This charity organisation was located at Lacombe in Alberta, Canada, where Keith lived. His association with the organisation secured additional funding for phase one of the school project to be built on land donated by Lilly's father.

A group of Canadian and Australian visitors to Kenya witnessed the opening of the Rapogi Lwanda Primary School in January, 2013. It comprised three classrooms, a teachers' office and bathrooms for students and teachers on a beautiful site that is fenced and gated.

Each year more buildings have been added, so that by 2022 the school had eight classrooms, an early childhood education cottage, a dormitory for 90 orphans, teachers' cottage, dining hall with new kitchen, and a deep well. On a nearby site there is a vocational centre and a large acreage for agriculture.

Importantly, the Rapogi Lwanda Primary School has achieved high success at the Grade 8 Kenya Certificate for Primary Education national examinations.

The school project speaks to a shared sensitivity, where a village community and all stakeholders combined to make a possibility become a reality. This included recognising human capital in the local community, a focus on small projects that could easily succeed, and sustainability—all under the umbrella of local community ownership.

The Rapogi Lwanda Primary School for Orphans, western Kenya. Top, classrooms, with dormitory on left; bottom, students at the school.

Our Kenyan daughter, Faith, has been joined by a group of orphans who have graduated from Grade 8 at Rapogi Lwanda and are studying at high schools and universities in Kenya. Faith graduated with a Diploma of Music from the University of Eastern Africa, Baraton in 2019 and is continuing to pursue a baccalaureate degree at Kabarak University.

Faith is becoming a specialist in African and Western Music, preparing her for a career as a teacher in Kenya.

There is another faith, a dynamic belief put into practice, which the people of this village in western Kenya share as they continue to build their primary school.

---

1 Delbert Baker, *From Exile to Prime Minister* (Washington, DC: Review and Herald Publishing Association, 1988).

2 Simon Robertson, "Nigeria's Deadly Days," *Time*, May 22, 2006, page 2.

6

THE THREE
PILLARS

The process of acquiring a PhD can inhibit normal conversation. The mind adapts to using esoteric terms that fit neatly in dissertations and professional journals but leave other audiences confused. And philosophy sometimes creeps into family conversations—a situation I can report from first-hand experience.

House hunting was near the top of our priorities upon our return to Australia after six years of travel, study and work abroad. There are many lakeside villages within a reasonable drive of the University of Newcastle. Silverwater was such a place, and the fact that it was located next to a suburb called Sunshine seemed a positive endorsement. Norene and I were excited to find a waterfront property at Silverwater.

The owners were two elderly women, and our scouting report indicated that they oscillated between "ready to sell" and "no way!" They were enthusiastic gardeners and would work themselves to the verge of a breakdown and decide to sell. But then the beloved garden needed care and why not plant some more? The cycle continued.

We visited the women on a day when they were ready to sell. They did. They then purchased a house nearby—and planted a garden.

The house at Silverwater was small and timber-framed. It would be easy to demolish. I was ready for the opportunity to plan a new residence on the waterfront, but my newfound academic philosophies almost let me down.

The most critical situation occurred when I talked aloud as I sketched our central living space. I should have let the sketch speak for itself—I was designing a living room. But I told Norene it was an existential platform in a garden. This is not the way to avoid client or wife problems.

Living rooms aside, a philosophical idea that resonates with me is the idea that there are three pillars in society—the home, church and school. The term "church" must be expanded to meet a diversity of forms. Yet, the pillars define the concepts of dwelling, worshipping and learning. Each is important as a philosophical underpinning and each has architectural implications.

The home

The architectural philosopher Christian Norberg-Schulz describes a conversation with his then 12-year-old son. When asked to tell something about his environment, his son replied, "Then I want to start with home, because it is from there, I go out to all the other places."[1] These words must have been music to his existentialist father's ears.

The home is a mainstay in society, offering protection and privacy to an individual or family. Human activities, even if seemingly trivialised, are the essence of creating a home.

This was emphasised when Norene and I visited London Zoo with our two young children. We had come early, but so had a multitude of other parents with children. We followed a group of them to the children's circus and, at the appointed time, a performance began. Just as it was becoming interesting, there was a terrible noise from across the walkway. It was music of sorts, amplified to the point of severe distortion.

I wondered how another activity in the grounds of the zoo could be permitted to interrupt the children's circus. The performance ended and we were curious to investigate the reason for the interruption. A large group of visitors was gathered around the fence to an enclosure where all was now quiet. We moved into position to see the exhibit. It was a middle-aged man in a business suit. We watched as he picked up his briefcase and walked away from a few pieces of living room furniture arranged on the grass. Several other settings were spread across the lawn all waiting for the presence of our human being.

The sign at the front of the exhibit read: "Urban man. *Homo sapiens urbanus*. This male is called ALBERTO VIDAL. He is on loan."

We, the spectators, were fascinated with Alberto. He didn't say a word. He read and snacked in a comfortable chair, changed into his pyjamas and brushed his teeth at the wash basin, lay on his bed, changed from pyjamas, sat at the breakfast table, and peddled an exercise bike. Then he returned to the "living room" and turned on the hi-fi—loud!

This was Alberto at home.

The design of a home for a family can take the analysis of human activities to a much more interesting level. Herman Hertzberger, a Dutch architect, was known for creating unfinished enclosures, leaving the completion of the spaces to the inhabitants. The inhabitants could tune the spaces in the way a violinist tunes his instrument.

I was fascinated to walk past a long line of two-storey apartments in Denbos, the Netherlands, where identically sized units fronted onto a suburban street. The architect, George Ang, had followed the lead of Hertzberger, giving the residents the opportunity to customise their entry precincts in ways that felt right to them.

In one entry precinct, there was easy access to the apartment door and an unobstructed view to the kitchen window. Another resident used the main material in the building's construction and provided a concrete block barbecue and storage bin. In another, the display of an expensive bicycle next to a herb garden said something about the life of this young professional.

There was a profusion of planting in one precinct, while in another a tall tree was paired with a stack of firewood ready for the coming winter. The function of the precinct was seen by another resident as a parking space, and they simply and unapologetically concreted the floor to park an Austin Mini.

The influence of culture can play a significant role in designing a home, and this may be seen in specific cultural traditions. Finland, for instance, preserves a sauna tradition that is best expressed historically as a separate building down a path from the home.

My first encounter with this sauna tradition began when I arrived in an isolated part of the Finnish countryside on a winter's night. I had been given directions to travel by bus and somehow managed to alight at the right farmhouse. My friend— an architect—would drive out from Helsinki to meet me the next day. But for the present, I was shuffling through snow to a doorway behind which three sisters and a brother were expecting me—their foreign visitor.

I soon found that none of my hosts for the night spoke any language familiar to me but this did not hinder their hospitality. After handshakes and refreshments, the brother led me outside towards a lake and into the sauna tradition.

The door opened to a small room—the first space within the sauna building. There was a fireplace in the corner, a wooden table and two benches, a clothes rack and a second door. The host put a match to the wood in the fireplace and turned to open a wooden shutter. Inside the wall, in front of a second shutter that could be opened to the winter outside, were several bottles. It was a neat refrigerator, and we sat at the table enjoying a cold drink.

The fire blazed enthusiastically, and the temperature increased in the small room. We stood to remove our coats. The conversation was of one or two words, repeated, interspersed with the periodic hanging of an article of clothing onto the clothes rack. It was a natural response to the rising temperature.

Forty minutes and another drink later, we closed the shutter to the drink closet, rose naked from the benches and opened the door to the second room. This was a bathroom with two copper kettles, two dishes and large pieces of soap hanging on the wall. There were three doors to this room. The sauna experience, as I had anticipated it, still lay ahead.

Fresh from bathing, we opened the door opposite the one through which we had entered, and there at last were the wooden slatted benches, a heat sink, ladle and a bucket of water. We used all of these, as well as hitting ourselves with birch branches to encourage circulation. The host passed the ladle to me so I could pour water onto the heat sink and control the intensity of the heatwaves that swept across the room.

After some time, we moved to the world outside, throwing snow at each other in the sub-zero temperature—but not for long. We soon returned to the sauna. The sequence of contrasts was exhilarating, and the periods of quietness inside the sauna became contemplative. I could now better understand my Finnish friends who had tried to explain that the sauna provided their most creative moments. One of the sisters later told me that she wrote poetry in the sauna, periodically opening a shutter to view the forest and lake.

The host and I went back to the bathroom. The dishes were emptied, and we returned to the first room. The remains of the fire glowed as we sat at the table, opened the shutter and brought out some bottles. The room was very warm from the heat generated in the closed space. During the next 30 minutes, the open "refrigerator" door and the dying embers cooled the space. It was a natural response to reach for our clothes and piece by piece we dressed. Eventually, we sat fully clothed at the table, just as we had done at the beginning of the sequence more than two hours before.

My reflections on this sauna experience first centred on the time taken to prepare for the ritual. During the afternoon, the fire had been laid and drinks brought to the first room. A generous supply of hot water had been stored in the kettles and wooden buckets in the second room. The stoking of the fire under the heat sink also required many trips to the sauna building during the afternoon.

I now understood how the Finnish sauna provides essential meanings within the geographic landscape of Finland, with its three elements of forests, rocks and lakes.

Finland is rich in forests of pine and birch. The sauna building is made of wood; the fire burns pine logs; and birch branches are cut at a certain time in summer. The sap will then hold the leaves intact for their winter use in the sauna. As well as being seen through open shutters in the summer, the presence of the forest is preserved in the sauna through the fragrance of burning wood and the dried birch leaves.

Scattered throughout the Finnish forests are granite rocks, which are used as the foundation of the sauna building and in broken form as the heat sink. They do not split when adding heat and water.

The presence of more than 60,000 lakes in Finland ensures that many saunas are ideally located at the edge of one. Water from the lake is poured onto the box of heated granite. Swimming in the lake is incorporated as part of the summer sauna experience.

Part of the tradition in Finland is to build the sauna as the first building on the home site. In a farm development, it could serve as bathroom, a place for drying fish or other meat and as a sick room when needed, due to its sterile environment.

There is another tradition related to the home, in which the brides and grooms of an isolated part of Scandinavia participate— but it doesn't involve a building. On one occasion, while arranging to take the ferry from Stockholm to Turku in western Finland, I chose a night passage so I could visit Mariehamn, the capital of the Åland Islands. The ship docked on a winter's morning and I ventured ashore while cargo was being unloaded. It was cold—minus 38 degrees cold, which is the same number whether measured in Celsius or Fahrenheit. I looked for a coffee shop or any open building as a place of shelter.

I was about to give up on my walking tour around the town when I came to the Åland Museum. The curator was opening its door, so I entered. It would take a while for my frozen jaw to operate, and I was pleased to simply look around.

A central exhibit was a wooden wagon. But it was a line of wooden objects about 45 centimetres (1.5 feet) tall, sitting under the wagon, that caught my attention. They looked rather like miniature women, each with a unique colourful ornament. The notice said: "Rockblåd." It sounded like a Swedish word and that made sense because the Åland Islands are closer to the coastal areas of Sweden than Finland. Swedish is the majority language, but the islands are remarkably independent while under Finnish sovereignty.

What were these objects displayed in a line?

The curator came by and I asked: "*Vad är rockblåd?*"

He described a tradition unique to the Åland Islands. In the year that a couple gets engaged, the groom makes a rockblåd for his future bride. He carves the "head" with a crown and heart. Then below, in the anatomical position of the heart, he includes something of special significance to the couple. The complete figure is supported by a single leg.

In addition to being a personal expression of love, the rockblåd has a function. Wool from an island farm is gathered and the bride-to-be twists this into a thread which is wound around the "waist" of the rockblåd as the groom turns it. The result of the shared process is a woven textile that the bride regularly wears.

I was impressed both by the decorative quality of the carving and the cultural tradition. As I indicated this, the curator expressed that it was impossible for a visitor to acquire what is a cultural relic. I understood. The rockblåd honoured the significant connection between a particular bride and groom. I moved on to other exhibits.

As I was preparing to leave, the curator came and reinforced his pleasure in my interest in the islands' cultural history. And perhaps there was a way for me to obtain a rockblåd. His friend Håkan was a craftsman who continued the carving tradition. Perhaps he could make one for me as a personal project—not as part of the Åland engagement tradition.

It happened. After a year, our rockblåd was completed, and it occupies a special place in our home. Håkan did not know of a personal motif for Norene, so he included a mirror in the "heart" position.

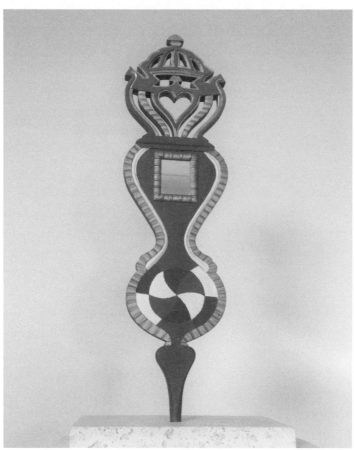

The rockblåd carved by sculptor Håkan for Neville and Norene Clouten, similar to cultural artifacts on display at the Åland Museum, Marienhaven, Åland Islands.

There are societies across the globe where marriage is culturally tied to the building of a house. The living space that two persons create becomes home—a main pillar of society.

Norberg-Schulz extends the thought but slips into words that are more associated with the existential. He concludes that when a space of love becomes public it gains the character of sacred space.[2]

The church

Synagogues, mosques and other sacred spaces provide a second pillar in society. This is certainly true for the Christian church.

Late one winter's afternoon, I made my way by public transport to a university campus set in a forest outside of Helsinki. It was already dark as I carried my suitcase across campus to a dormitory. I was weary and sleep came easily. The next thing I knew, the sun was shining through the window and I heard the distant, repetitive sound of hammers driving nails into wood. I arose and soon made my way to the ground floor exit.

As I rounded the corner of the dormitory, I could scarcely believe my eyes. The Otaniemi Chapel was being built. The reason for my surprise was that I had visited the completed chapel several times during the two previous decades. But here it was being built—again!

In 1957, Kaija and Heikki Siren received first prize in a design competition for this university chapel. Their building served the campus community well. Then one morning the Lutheran church pastor telephoned the architect's office.

"You know the building you designed 20 years ago? It burned down last night. Get out the plans. We want to build it again. No changes."

There were many options available to the client: hire another architect; initiate a process to introduce improvements based on experience; achieve a building to speak specifically to contemporary issues, and so on. But no!

No changes.

However, the approach to the chapel was not the same as it had once been. Other buildings had encroached upon it.

Back in the 1960s, I followed the path towards the chapel as it left a meadow and entered the forest. There was scent from the moss and ground cover. I stopped to pick some blueberries, then continued on. The path turned a corner and there was the rising form of the chapel with its courtyard and bell tower.

As I arrived at the opening in the wall of this precinct, I felt the experience of leaving the forest. Five low steps spilled out towards me and I climbed them—one, two, three, four, five. Kaija and Heikki Siren had designed a definite threshold to the church precinct.

Inside the precinct, I was surrounded by human-scale enclosures. Ahead, past four columns to the tower, was the wall of the chapel. I approached the entrance door—another threshold—then I experienced being in the chapel. The altar, lectern, font and communion rail were statements of simplicity in design and steel construction, all placed in front of a glass wall to the forest.

Otaniemi Chapel at the Helsinki University of Technology, Espoo, Finland. Designed by architects Kaija and Heikki Siren. Completed 1957, rebuilt 1978.

A cross was located 9 metres (30 feet) outside the glass, just in front of the trees.

Through this sequence of experiences, I had reached the goal set by the client's program and the architect's intentions. As a willing participant, I knew where I was at each location on the journey's path. It reminds me of a statement of Roberto Gerhard, "Form in music means knowing at every moment exactly where one is."[3] In music and architecture, there is both path and goal.

The Otaniemi Chapel was rebuilt to honour the original creative process, and the building created twice speaks to the timeless quality of its architecture.

There is another example of this rare quality—in a North American forest. It is interesting that once again the chapel experience focuses on a cross outside, located within the forest.

The architect, E Fay Jones, designed the Thorncrown Chapel near Eureka Springs, Arkansas. It was completed in 1980. A paved

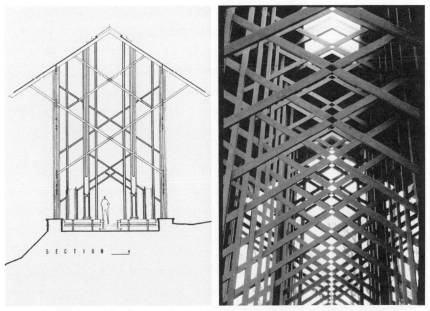

SECTION

Thorncrown Chapel, Eureka Springs, Arkansas. Designed by architect E Fay Jones. Completed 1980. The image on the left shows the simplicity of the architect's design; the right is a photograph of the interior experienced as a celebration.

path from the parking area gently curves among the trees. It was along this original track that two workmen carried all the "two by fours" and larger timber sections to the site. With sensitivity and care, the building elements were assembled.

Glass walls between the timber structure celebrate the trees, leaving the beauty of the site intact. The only steel used was in the form of small diamond-shaped connectors to hold the wooden trusses. '

The American Institute of Architects includes the Thorncrown Chapel in its list of the 10 most significant buildings of the 20th century.

The Hillview Seventh-day Adventist Church in Australia has a much more conventional design for a worship space, but still has an intentional visual sequence on entry. I included a low concrete beam in the structure as a threshold to the church sanctuary. Attention is directed to a white woollen carpet fixed high on a tower wall. Then, in the original design, the worshipper's experience is drawn down to a group of pottery cups, a jug and platter on a bench. The combination of the white "towel" and the communion "table" are important Christian symbols.

The process of designing a church building lends itself to collaboration between worshippers and the architect. I have incorporated user-participation workshops in several church architectural projects.

A weekend workshop for a church in Queensland led the congregation, with my input, to propose two entry precincts on different sides of the site and at different levels. The participants in the workshop used magazine cut-outs, cereal squares and parsley to share ideas for an outdoor space where church members could mingle with visitors. The group used the term *agora*—a public space—for this friendship courtyard under trees. They proposed a more conventional entry to their worship space at right angles to the courtyard.

I sketched the plans of the two entry levels as discussed in the user-participation workshop and sent them with some text to the editor of a church journal. I devoted much of the text to describing the *agora* concept and how the natural environment and the inclusion of tables and benches would create the outdoor "friendship space."

When I received a copy of the journal, I was surprised to find that the editor had cropped the plan of the "friendship space" so that only the walls of the church remained. I suspect the thought was, "What are all these trees and benches for? We don't need that!"

There are great opportunities to design environments for worship to meet both practical aspects of following a spiritual path and of being part of a richness in worship experience.

The school

Many creative design projects do not get to see the light of day. Not so with a building in northern Tasmania. It is an early learning centre, and it serves to introduce the third pillar in society—the school.

The Bungawitta Early Learning Centre in the north of Launceston takes its name from an Aboriginal word meaning "a place of little possums." The architect for the 1986 building was Robert Morris-Nunn.

A clue to the creativity of the design found in the building can be seen at the entrance. It looks like the front of a little house, complete with two square four-paned windows, a door and an angled chimney—just like a child's drawing of a house.

The building is of a similar size to large houses in the suburban area. It could have been a home-pattern school, where learning spaces are created in the scale of a home. But it goes far beyond that to use the village as a model.

Stepping into the early learning centre, you enter a downtown Launceston street of miniature one- and two-storey buildings, with doors, windows, roof eaves and balconies built to the dimensions of children. A glass roof pours daylight onto the street.

The small reception area is under the clock tower of the first building—the miniature Bungawitta Post Office. The counter in the reception space, when seen from a child's perspective, is a small pet shop with a display window through which children see goldfish swimming. It is the building's introduction to the small child who clings to a parent's leg during the registration process.

Walking down the colourful street of shop fronts, the child passes "Cockatoo Cove," "Platypus Place" and "Echidna Nook." There is a bank, traffic markings on the roadway and a park with a potted kumquat tree. The park doubles as a tiny courtyard where two or three adults can sit adjacent to the staff room and drink coffee. At the end of the street is a petrol station with a miniature pump for "Possum Petrol," a stand for "Bunga Tyres" and a bench

Bungawitta Early Learning Centre, Newnham, Tasmania. Designed by architect Robert Morris-Nunn. Completed 1986.

with a cash register. There are doors from the street into school rooms for a variety of large and small group activities.

It is the direct relationship between the dimensions of people and the dimensions of the places they inhabit and the objects they use that begins to define human scale. Bungawitta illustrates this superbly.

My teaching career has been with students at the other end of their education. As a professor, the need to prepare lectures on architecture has often provided reasons for travel. One can read and look at plans and illustrations, but it is the personal experience gained from visiting historic and contemporary built environments that can best supplement lectures and studio discussions.

The death of Alvar Aalto—one of the masters of modern architecture—gave me a reason to make travel plans to go back to Finland in 1978. I was interested in what effect Aalto's death might have on the younger generation of Finnish architects. I also thought the subject would be of interest to editors of international architectural journals. This proved to be the case.

My first excursion brought me to Helsinki in the northern winter. I stayed in a room designed by Aalto with a splayed geometry, and I became a regular patron for dinner each evening at Reima Pietila's non-rectilinear Dipoli building.

I spent a lot of time at the Museum of Finnish Architecture. The curator was interested in my research and we shared several morning-tea discussions. I was becoming more familiar with the work of younger Finnish architects, but I suspected that Reima Pietila was most likely to slip into the space left by Aalto. It would be enlightening to talk to Pietila. The difficulty was how to meet him.

The curator knew his weekly schedule. He would fly to Kuwait each Sunday, where major government projects and the Sief Palace were under construction. On Wednesday, he would be in his office in Helsinki, and he would take the night train to Oulu, above the Arctic Circle. He was professor and dean of the School of Architecture at the University of Oulu. On Friday, he would return to Helsinki to begin the weekly cycle again.

His busy schedule meant that Helsinki was not the place to attempt a rendezvous. Oulu would perhaps be possible. I also wanted to visit Aalto's buildings at Rovaniemi, even further north than Oulu. A visit to these two towns on an eight-day train pass seemed doable. I took the risk to meet Pietila.

Arriving in Oulu from Rovaniemi on Wednesday night, I carried my bag to a hotel only a few blocks from the School of Architecture. Early next morning, I was speaking with the secretary when a small man with a coat and cap walked in.

It had to be Reima Pietila.

We had a few minutes before he said it was time for his lecture and I would be welcome to attend. The topic was the American architect Louis Kahn, and every 10 minutes or so I was given a few sentences in English. The slides were of buildings known to me.

The lecture was a full morning event and I chatted with Pietila for 15 minutes afterwards. Then a Japanese student arrived, and we were both invited to a fine restaurant for dinner that evening. The student had studied Pietila's work in the third year of his architecture program in Tokyo and had come to Oulu to continue his study. He quickly learned Finnish and was a special student to the professor.

The assistant dean also joined us for dinner. He had a few questions for Pietila, and these were addressed. My questions then monopolised the discussions and the hours ticked by. During the evening, I heard the names of many younger architects, and on some occasions, I asked for these names to be written down so that I would have the correct spelling. These architects would be added to my list back at the museum.

It was close to midnight when Pietila, the Japanese student and I left the restaurant. The assistant dean had left some time earlier. Not a word was spoken as we walked in the minus 40-degree temperature.

I had heard from the Japanese student that he lived across town in student housing. We were now walking in the opposite direction and I tried to query this. But the student simply gestured that he was staying with the professor to see him home. When we reached Pietila's hotel, we stopped at the corner of the building, said goodnight, and the student walked with the professor to the hotel entrance door.

I thought it was a great mark of respect for the professor, and I was not sure if I had witnessed a Finnish or Japanese tradition. The student and I set off for my hotel—again not in the direction of the student housing. My attempt to say goodbye did not register with the student, and I realised that now I was the old man, and he would walk with me to my hotel.

I was ready to collapse as the hotel clerk opened the door. As I went upstairs, I thought of the Japanese student still walking. But it was my frozen feet that kept me awake.

The night finally ended, and I made my way to the secretary's desk at the School of Architecture. I had checked out of the hotel, thinking it would be a good idea to leave my bag at the office while I took a few photographs of the town.

The secretary was ready to meet me.

"The professor is not coming in. He has a bad cold."

My thought that I was responsible for the late night was interrupted by the next sentence: "The professor asked if you would take the lecture this morning."

I would, and I did. In English, with key words written on the blackboard.

That one night and morning began a close relationship with the architect and educator who filled the space left by Alvar Aalto.

The school at whatever level is an important pillar that combines with the home and church in societies far and wide.

1 Christian Norberg-Schulz, *Existence, Space and Architecture* (London: Studio Vista, 1971), page 9.

2 ibid, page 34.

3 Roberto Gerhard, "The nature of music," *The Score*, 16, 1956, page 7; quoted in Yi-Fu Tuan, *Space and Place: The Perspective of Experience* (Minneapolis: University of Minnesota Press, 1977), page 15.

7

ANDREWS UNIVERSITY

My brother and I walked home along the path from the Toronto Public School, New South Wales, and crossed the creek in front of our house. Our parents met us with excited faces and Dad was holding a letter. It was from the Sanitarium Health Food Company in response to an inquiry made a few years before. He had asked if he might be contacted should work become available at the factory.

The reason was education. Their two boys, then six and eight years of age, were students at the local public school but this was not our parents' dream. The plan was for Christian education and to them that meant the Seventh-day Adventist primary and high schools on the campus of Avondale College. It meant leaving our Stoney Creek address and moving to Cooranbong, where the schools and the Sanitarium factory were located.

I was reminded of this imperative for Christian education decades later while in a rural village in Kenya. As mentioned in the essay on Africa, my wife and I were there for quite another reason, but the men of the village believed their dream for a school was about to be realised. We had surely come to help them build their school.

It is not surprising that the theme of architecture runs through the essays in this book. But education has also been a significant theme in my life. It was education—both receiving and giving— that led me from Avondale Primary School in Cooranbong, Australia to be the Inaugural Professor of Architecture at Andrews University in Berrien Springs, Michigan.

In my high school years, the choice of subjects was actually not a choice at all. Boys took science; girls took art. I wanted to take both. A few boys were not interested in science, so a third subject was offered—technical drawing. The administration must have believed that this would solve the problem and still keep the genders separated. I wanted to take all three subjects. However, I joined the boys who enrolled in the technical drawing option. There was a new teacher, Adrian Ellison, and he became my first mentor.

Two experiences in the technical drawing class were important to me. A friend of Adrian's asked for help in designing and drawing plans for a house. This opportunity was passed on to me.

Then one afternoon as the class commenced, I was told that the director of the engineering drawing office at the Sanitarium factory wanted to see me after school. The interview led to work at the drawing office for a few hours after school several days each week and during summer vacations.

I was privileged to attend the University of Sydney under the Commonwealth Scholarship program, then to supplement the Australian professional degree in architecture with a master's degree from North America and a doctorate from Edinburgh.

This preparation through education led to Andrews University and the opportunity to create and direct the only program in architecture within the global reach of Seventh-day Adventist education.

A small group of Adventist architects came together to form the Department of Architecture in August, 1980. The objective was to gain national accreditation for a program that would graduate architects for practice within and beyond the global mission of the

Seventh-day Adventist Church, providing a Christian context for creative endeavours.

Two innovations were introduced into the Andrews University architectural curriculum. The early years of the program were organised around integrated studies. Extensions from the arts, physics and the social sciences were team-taught in hands-on studios of discovery. The second innovation was the inclusion of artistry as a measure of professional competence, and this was introduced in the final years of the program. We used the term reflective practice for this inclusion of artistry. The focus on creativity in the program meant that studio projects were often taught with the allied disciplines of interiors and landscape design.

The National Architectural Accrediting Board accepted the validity of an architectural program with a Christian focus as part of the diversity of programs in North America. Full accreditation of five years for the Bachelor of Architecture program was granted in 1987. It was the only new architecture program accredited in the 1980s.

Andrews University enjoys a large representation of international students, and this is extremely valuable in the study of architecture. Differences in culture were celebrated in mission projects in South America and Africa. The philosophy was to bend the knee in humility and stand tall in service. The global legacy of the Department of Architecture outreach continues to this day and enriches the education of architects and designers.

The faculty of the program were mainly architectural practitioners and took every opportunity to supplement theoretical knowledge and applications in studio projects with field trips to significant examples of the built environment and to practitioners' offices.

A chapter of Tau Sigma Delta, the national honour society for architecture and the allied arts, was inaugurated. So too was a student chapter of the American Institute of Architects. Students were enthusiastic, and sometimes surprised faculty with their creativity.

A film promotes creativity

To fundraise for the fledgling chapter of the American Institute of Architects, students hired a 35-mm projector and promoted a community-wide film evening in the university gymnasium. I suggested the film *Dersu Uzala*—a foreign film with English subtitles.

Set in Siberia, the story begins in 1909. A surveyor, who is also a captain in the Russian army, has been given the task of obtaining surveying information from landmarks near a lake in the northern reaches of the tundra. The soldiers assigned to the captain carry provisions and surveying equipment. This includes a theodolite to record angles to natural landmarks.

The film introduces a campsite in the forest. The evening meal has ended, and the group relaxes around the fire. One by one the soldiers go to sleep. Soon it is only the captain who is awake, writing in his diary, and then he too gives in to drowsiness. Suddenly, the camp is interrupted by a sound from the forest. The soldiers reach for their guns, ready for the entry of a bear. Instead, there is a voice.

"Don't shoot!"

Into the story walks a nomadic hunter clothed in animal skins. The soldiers share the remnants of the evening's stew. Then a brief conversation begins with a question as to the visitor's identity.

He responds, "My name is Dersu. Dersu Uzala. I am a hunter."

As the captain reclines to sleep, he muses on the value of having a nomadic hunter as a member of his team. Clearly, the knowledge of the topography and landscape will be significant. The next morning an invitation to Dersu is offered and accepted. The film then presents a sequence of events in which the hunter is shown to be perceptive to the natural environment and sensitive to the needs of others. By way of contrast, the soldiers are neither.

The days become weeks, and incidents multiply. Eventually, the last base camp is established. The summer is rapidly coming to an end and the only remaining objective is to walk to the shore of a northern lake, take a survey bearing with the theodolite, and return home before winter. The Siberian excursion has taken longer than projected and, to save time, the captain and Dersu set out for the lake, leaving the soldiers and provisions at the camp.

The captain leads the way and, as the afternoon progresses, Dersu shares an increasing concern for a change in the weather. He strongly urges a return to base camp. However, the captain is close to realising the surveying objective—the main reason for the summer's expedition. They press on and finally reach the shore of the lake.

Just as they open the tripod and focus the telescope of the theodolite onto an important landmark, a first rush of wind arrives. Dersu has remained loyal to his leader all day, but now his fears for an early blizzard compel him to take control. He orders the captain to cut bundles of the reeds that define the water's edge, and by example wields his own long knife. They both work as if their lives depend on it. Dersu knows that they do.

The blizzard increases its fury and several times the film catches a glimpse of the captain falling to the ground through the driven snow. Dersu is always nearby to shout orders. The captain somehow summons the little remaining energy from his exhausted reservoir. Eventually, he fails to respond to the call.

The camera portrays the drama of the blizzard. Then, after a short pause, it reveals a northern sunrise across a tranquil landscape of soft mottled white. The beauty of the morning is revealed as the camera pans the landscape. It comes to rest at a shelter of reeds covered with windswept snow. Then a crack on the shelter's curved wall develops into a door. Dersu emerges, takes in the setting, and pokes his head back inside the shelter.

"Wake up, captain."

Opening his eyes, the captain sees the inside of a conical space made from reeds bound into sheaths. Filled with amazement, he is more appreciative of Dersu than ever. The nomadic hunter has saved his life. They stand together beside the shelter, then Dersu begins to tear it apart. He reaches into the mass of reeds and snow and extracts the surveying tripod that had provided the structural support.

The students enjoyed the film—and even more its ability to raise funds for a visit to New York City. In due course, the plans for the field trip turned into reality, and we set off early one morning shoe-horned into a university van and towing a small trailer laden with sleeping bags and sacks of various description. En route, along the Pennsylvania Turnpike, conversations ended suddenly with a flat tyre on the trailer. My teaching associate and I set out in the van, leaving the group of students and the disabled trailer in a bleak and windy landscape.

Eventually a tyre of the unusually small size required was found and purchased, and we began the return journey to the trailer location. As we approached, there were no students in sight. Then we saw them!

In a carefully selected place was an example of American vernacular architecture that would have warmed the heart of any teacher of art or writer on culture. A shelter had been constructed with a few strong sticks and all manner of "trash," which had been collected from a stretch of the turnpike. Pieces of plastic, rubber, cardboard and wood were interwoven to form both windbreak and roof. The shelter's silhouette included willow sticks donned with drink cans that reached out to the sky like antennae. And there were Dersu-like bundles of grass. The students sat cross-legged beneath the structure facing the road, well pleased with their initiative to protect themselves from the wind and showers. It was a worthwhile outcome for a three-hour delay in the journey.

Another memory is from the beginning of a visit to Australia with 22 Andrews University students. We could not leave the airport at Papeete, Tahiti during a stopover of several hours in the middle of the night, so we gathered near a large tree inside the terminal. In our carry-on baggage we each had a sketchbook, and with improvised brushes and a collective cup of coffee, we added soft "sepia" washes to pen sketches of the tree. The result was a collection of fine watercolours.

The visit to Australia gave us confidence to offer a full semester of studios in Finland and to develop themes for designing a variety of building types on continents with diverse cultures and climates.

Environments for worship

Beyond the Department of Architecture, I appreciated the opportunity to team-teach a course on "Architecture for Worship" in the Theological Seminary.

As information on the Andrews University program in architecture reached churches in North America, I received many invitations to meet with building committees and church groups. Such visits provided opportunities to hone ideas for an emerging theology of environments for worship. These ideas were discussed with faculty and Honours students and shared in church publications and secular print.

I was also pleased to lead hands-on workshops for church groups who were designing new buildings. These workshops—with an architect as facilitator—can bring a congregation together in a creative endeavour. The focus is on a design journey to an outcome of meaningful worship. Activities over a weekend might include an awareness walk—even to a well-known building site—worship, then a day where a collection of everyday objects is gathered to make models. Cut-outs and colour patches from magazines give mood, cereal squares become chairs, and parsley is used for vegetation. Themes develop that will lead to discussions towards possible points of consensus. There is a need, however, for church groups to follow through with a strong commitment.

Prior to my years at Andrews University, I visited North America on several occasions. I was attracted to a photograph of a church model published in a journal. It was small, and the accompanying text was short. It mentioned that the church had held a design workshop with an architect to develop the plans for their new building. Although the location of this church in northern California was a day's drive from where I was, the photograph of the model and brief information was sufficient for me to rent a car.

It was late afternoon when I arrived at the town and I chose to visit the architect's office before it closed. As I entered the foyer, I noted that the well-crafted model of the church was on display. It was somewhat concerning that the model was there rather than on display at the new church.

The architect quickly established that the project had been shelved. A member of the church's building committee said that he could build the church for less. And he did.

I drove to the church and, as I entered, an elderly woman came to meet me. Hearing the reason for my visit, she opened her handbag and removed a worn copy of the photograph and text I recognised.

"I don't think we got this church here, do you?" she said.

Then she put the piece of paper back in her handbag, to be again carried around as a reminder of a workshop she had enjoyed and a building that might have been.

I suggest that the first objective for designing worship spaces is to be creative; the second is to design well. When designing a building for worship, it is important to think about what it is that we want our church buildings to say. I believe they should respond uniquely to our beliefs.

Then there is the need to build well. The design quality of Shaker furniture is recognised both for the conceptual thinking that occurred in the design process and the high standard of workmanship during construction. Church buildings should do the same.

Truth can be expressed in honest and authentic ways in the choice of building materials and in craftsmanship. Harold Best, in his essay *God's Creation and Human Creativity*, refers to the contemporary division between worth and function. In contrast, "every speck" of God's handiwork "is lovingly made....There is no model whatsoever in the Creation for a division between worth and function, or immediacy and timelessness."[1]

As worshippers of a creative God, we are provided the opportunity to "imagine, to construct, to rise above our environments and to change them, to order them, to delight in their endless variety."[2] These words of Ottilie Stafford are offered with the idea that human participation with the Creator in the creative process "is itself a form of worship." She goes on to say: "Worship involves experiences and expressions quite apart from the practical, utilitarian, rational expressions of our ordinary life." The title of Ottilie's paper is appropriately "The Holiness of Beauty: Why Imagination matters." Similarly, Ed Sovik describes beauty as "the metaphor of the Holy."[3]

Given the outcome of enrichment through wide participation that we seek in creating places of worship, everyone who is willing to participate in the process of designing a church should do so. The poet, philosopher, physicist, soup kitchen worker and high school student—all can share visionary and most unexpected ideas in the design process.

The following approach to designing a church parallels the definition of creativity described by Paul Torrance as "the process of sensing problems or gaps in information, forming ideas and hypotheses, testing and modifying these hypotheses, and communicating the results."[4] It is summarised in the diagram on the next page.

The process begins with perceptive inquiry—or perceiving needs. In order to find design solutions, we first need to understand what problems and needs a building should address. Following this analysis, information and postulates are brought together into synthesis proposals.

This is where the involvement of as many individuals as possible is stimulating to those who participate and potentially rewarding to the outcome. Some suggestions may appear to derive from unleashed imagination, but this divergence within the community is important to creativity. Divergence is valid providing the ideas do not go on to be built without proper evaluation.

I suggest that architects lead the way in eliminating fanciful notions—and perhaps some traditionally accepted ones—that

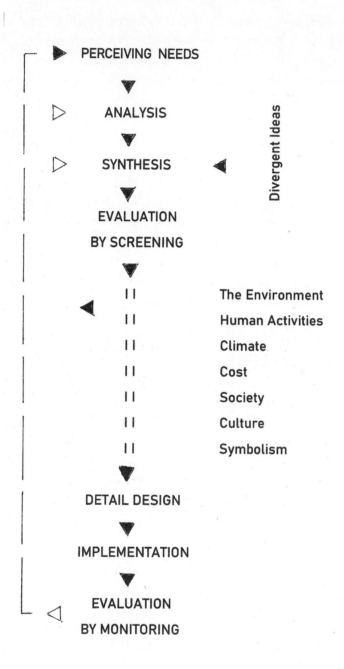

Process for designing. Published in Neville Clouten, "Architecture of Participation," Adventist Review, September 22, 1988, pages 16–18.

should not be built. All synthesis proposals from the broad, turbulent ocean of ideas must be sieved as objectively as possible. Only a proposal that can pass through the filtering tests is worth developing and implementing. It is here that an unexpected idea may come through the process and lead to innovation in architecture.

The diagram suggests seven sieves—or filters—for the evaluation of proposals and as a means of identifying appropriate church architecture.[5] The first filter is the appropriateness of a proposed building in the context of its surrounding environment. The other filters are the human activity needs that initiated the design process, then climate, cost, society, culture and symbolism. These filters are discussed in more detail below.

The architect develops the selected proposal and uses models, drawings and specifications to refine the building's design. During implementation, the client would expect the architect to exercise strict cost control within contractual procedures.

An important final phase is the assessment of the building in use over a period of time. User-evaluation studies compare the actual use of space with the original objectives and client expectations. The design process then becomes circular, providing information back to the perception, analysis and synthesis proposals associated with another design project.

Creativity is a cooperative, ongoing process that is all-inclusive.

Seven filters for identifying appropriate church architecture

1. The environment

The first filter is the environment. A forest setting may lead to a building very different from one developed with sensitivity in an urban environment.

The worship space of the Temppeliaukio church in Helsinki is cut from a rock outcrop, and for generations the acropolis site has been surrounded by apartment houses. The church building, designed by Timo and Tuomo Suomalainen and completed in 1969, preserves the openness of the setting and continues the opportunities for public access onto the outcrop. A small metal cross is bolted to the rock near the church entrance.

The experience inside the church combines a sense of security in a space subtracted from the bedrock and a sense of unification under a shallow, domed ceiling. Inclined areas of roof glazing adjust the irregularities of the rock walls to the exact geometry of the dome. In winter, candles flicker on the natural rock shelves and thin copper ceiling strips reflect all available light. Imagine the voices of a male choir filling the reverberant space.

Another outstanding example is St Peter's Lutheran Church in New York City, designed by Hugh Stubbins. The church is a "good neighbour" to surrounding buildings, yet at the same time it is set apart. It holds its own on the site of the high-rise Citicorp office tower, the development of which necessitated the replacement of a church building.

Temppeliaukio, Helsinki, Finland. Designed by architects Timo and Tuomo Suomalainen. Completed 1969.

Exterior cross (top) and interior (bottom) of Temppeliaukio, Helsinki, Finland. Designed by architects Timo and Tuomo Suomalainen. Completed 1969.

The new church, while dwarfed by the tower, is in scale with a gathering place where people may stop, communicate and rest in the outdoors. From the street, the passer-by can see into the worship space.

This church is in the world and for the world, but it preserves its integrity. A change in geometric form sets it apart from the towering rectilinear buildings for banking and commerce.

2. Human activities

Buildings provide spatial enclosures for human activities. The Emmanuel's Church in Jönköping, Sweden, is a replacement building in a historic area of timber buildings. The limited site and a large program of community needs precluded a generous entry courtyard, so the architect Carl Nyren designed a small octagonal space next to the street. It welcomes all to enter anytime during the long hours that the building is open. Seats near the separate entrances to the church and social centre are under a central tree. The emphasis on human needs continues into the foyer, where one first sees a table with provisions for hot and cold drinks. People naturally respond by placing a few kronor on the counter, taking up a cup and pastry, and moving to a nearby chair.

3. Climate

There are several principles that guide the design of churches in relation to climate. These include the selection of a site and the building's orientation, the inclusion of sun screening, lighting, ventilation and solar technologies. Locations in very cold climates require the physical separation of exterior forms from the interior building structure.

Swedish architect Ralph Erskine suggests that towns and buildings could open "like flowers to the sun of spring and summer but, also like flowers, turn their backs on the shadows and cold northern winds, offering sun-warmth and wind-protection."6

4. Cost

Central to the design of appropriate environments is cost. Even a building with a large budget should convey a message of accountability. Fortunately, design quality does not depend on large budgets. Low-cost churches with simplicity in plan and built with standard off-the-shelf components may include a small courtyard with a profusion of planting.

An example is a church that burned to the ground. Almost immediately a building committee was formed, and members interviewed three architects. The one chosen suggested a user-participation workshop, and church members met for two days in a tent on the site. An awareness walk on the first morning created real interest in a small area with shrubs that had been preserved. It was decided this would be a prayer garden and it became the centre for outdoor fellowship. It provided a luxury of plants at low cost.

5. Society

Concern for individual and community needs and cost-accountable architecture can lead to environmental design for the whole of society. This includes all aspects of structural safety, non-toxic materials and barrier-free design. The Christian must take every opportunity to support society's health and happiness. In many ways, Christians follow the physician's diagnostic role, perceiving areas of stress and relieving tensions.

The Finnish architect Alvar Aalto suggested that "there are many situations in life in which the organisation is too brutal; it is the task of the architect to give life a gentler structure."[7] The statement was made in 1955 and challenges us today to design churches of a gentler architecture.

6. Culture

Church building design should also respond to culture. The geographic, historic and societal contexts may combine into a spirit of place, or *genius loci*, to create a distinct character. This was understood by the architect Don Gazzard in his design for the Wentworth Memorial Church in Vaucluse, close to Sydney Harbour. The elements of *genius loci*—paths and places that create domains for human interaction—are illustrated in the way the church is approached.

It is located at the end of a narrow path that climbs to a sandstone outcrop on the top of a ridge. The path ends at a threshold to a forecourt, occupying half of the small irregular site. An elevated paved area towards the church building provides a second threshold to the door of the church, located beneath an extension to the roof. In all the details, the pedestrian approach is consistent with the hillside and the houses oriented towards the harbour.

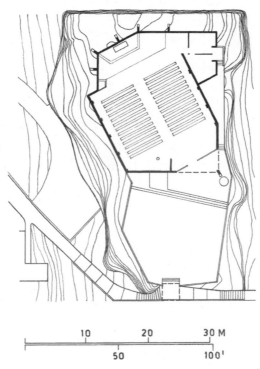

Plan of the Wentworth Memorial Church, Vaucluse, New South Wales. Designed by architect Don Gazzard. Completed 1965.

Wentworth Memorial Church, Vaucluse, New South Wales. Designed by architect Don Gazzard. Completed 1965. Top, entry porch; bottom, forecourt, with the entrance to the church on the right.

The church was completed in 1965 and was heritage-listed in 2012, both for its architecture and as a memorial to the local service men and women who served in World War II. In spite of expressions of concern, the property has been in and out of new ownership. The building remains intact. Its sales and potential sales have moved from funeral operator, to hotelier, to use as a private residence with a basement lap pool.

7. Symbolism

The last of the seven filters for appropriate architecture is symbolism. The Canberra National Seventh-day Adventist Church, Australia, designed by architect Ken Woolley of Ancher, Mortlock and Woolley, integrates water in its design as a symbol for baptism. Triangular buttresses rise from a large pool within the courtyard. Worshippers enter the church at a level beneath the waterline. Inside, to one side of the pulpit, a cylindrical baptismal font bathed in light further emphasises the significance of baptism.

Art and architectural history provide a vocabulary of symbolic forms and spaces. St Peters Lutheran Church, Columbus, Indiana introduces symbolism in the selection of geometries for the plan of the church. Designed in 1988 by Gunnar Birkerts, the interior plan has two circles, superimposed against a rectilinear geometry on one side. There is a sense of containment in the smaller circle, which has seating for 320 in close association with the worship centre. The larger circle adds a thousand seats on a rising level around and above the inner circle.

Worshippers come together as a group within a circle, and they also seek direction by turning towards a lectern for the spoken Word. Birkerts described the symbolism in the church plan, saying, "Togetherness and direction are in the concept of the plan."[8]

Designers of contemporary churches are able to select from an array of Christian symbols to convey meaning. Common objects such as the towel, water, the cup and bread took on special meaning as they were used in New Testament times and as they pointed to a second advent. A focus on the end of the journey does not need to limit how the creative process and aesthetics can enrich the journey. We are able to do both.

Practicing architects serve on juries for student projects. Beyond this, leading practitioners join with architectural educators to serve on juries to identify examples of the built environment worthy of receiving design awards. Most of these are given by the Institute of Architects soon after the completion of a building. They can speak to a positive relationship between a client and architect. But jury comments may not be considered important to some members of a church congregation. These members may have an appreciation or otherwise for their place of worship and have no need for more than that. Other worshippers see themselves as informed clients and have insights into the design of churches that enrich their worship experience.

The commentary of design professionals, whether as jurors or written in publications, can heighten this. At the extreme, there may be theorists who use esoteric language and speak only to their own group. Hopefully, it is more common to have critiques that heighten worshippers' awareness of why and how the experience of their church is enriching them.

The Canberra National Seventh-day Adventist Church, mentioned earlier, received a design award when completed in 1971. The Royal Australian Institute of Architects Awards Committee visited this new church and presented the award in recognition of its architectural significance. The jury commended the design of the entry courtyard, which includes a view of the Lutheran church tower next door. It is a good example of the Japanese principle of borrowing a landscape. Of more importance to the jury was the summary of the clients' intent and expectations. Twenty-five years later, these statements were the basis for another visit.

The most prestigious award of many architectural institutes is the 25-year award. This is the case for the Royal Australian Institute of Architects, and the award is titled the Enduring Architecture

Canberra National Seventh-day Adventist Church, Australia. Designed by architect Ken Woolley of Anchor Mortlock Murray and Woolley. Completed 1971. Awarded the 25-year Enduring Architecture Award by Royal Australian Institute of Architects in 1996. Top, exterior; bottom, interior.

Award. A visit by the Enduring Architecture Awards committee took place in 1996. These jurors recognised the architectural significance of the building when designed, but more importantly they assessed how its continued significance had demonstrated its "enduring" qualities over the 25-year period. The jury noted:

> The design of the church combines concepts in contemporary church architecture with a symbolic design which reflects the beliefs of the SDA congregation.... The use of light and water highlight key elements of the doctrine. Light falls from high windows, reflects into the church from a pool outside the church, is focused on the baptismal font, and is emphasised by the white of the walls.

The jury commented on the water level at the entry and how "the prominent and unusual baptismal font highlights the key role of baptism by immersion."

A citation of the Enduring Architecture Award is exhibited on a bronze plaque in the church entry. In the summary of the Statement of Significance there is this sentence:

> The architecture of the church may contribute to the education of designers in their understanding of the development of Late Twentieth Century architectural styles.

It seems to me that these statements take us back to the academic setting of Andrews University. The architect at the Canberra church took the theology we wanted to communicate, and both educators and practitioners were pleased with how the building connected with the beliefs.

1 Harold M Best, "God's Creation and Human Creativity," in *The Reality of Christian Learning: Strategies for Faith-Discipline Integration*, editors Harold Heie and David Wolfe (St Paul: Christian University Press, 1987), page 263.

2 Ottilie Stafford, "The Holiness of Beauty: Why Imagination Matters," *Spectrum*, 7(4), 1975, page 10.

3 Ed Sovik, "The Mirror of the Church," *Faith and Form: Journal of the Interfaith Forum of Religion Art and Architecture,* Fall, 1988, page 17.

4 Paul Torrance, *Creativity* (Washington, DC: National Education Association of the United States, 1963), page 3.

5 Neville Clouten, "Architecture of Enrichment," *Adventist Review*, September 15, 1988, pages 18–23; and "Architecture of Participation," *Adventist Review*, September 22, 1988, pages 16–18.

6 Ralph Erskine, *The Polar Record* (Cambridge, England: The Scott Research Institute, 1968), quoted in Peter Collymore, *The Architecture of Ralph Erskine* (London: Granada, 1982), page 26.

7 Cited in Aarno Ruusuvuori (Editor), *Alvar Aalto* (Helsinki: Museum of Finnish Architecture, 1978), page 50.

8 Design statement in association with Kay Kaiser, "Another Jewel in the Crown: St Peter's Church, Columbus, Indiana," *Faith and Form: Journal of the Interfaith Forum on Religion, Art and Architecture*, Winter 1988–89, pages 9–13.

8

HOMECOMING

It was a dream come true. In August, 2003, Norene and I were aboard the *Queen Elizabeth II* as it called at ports along the Norwegian coastline and cruised into fjords. The next day we would arrive at Ålesund. As we returned to our cabin after dinner, a flashing light alerted us that there was a message on the telephone.

We would be met at the wharf by some of Norene's relatives. The message made it clear that we were conscripted to them for the day. As we left the ship the next morning, we were greeted with a large placard held high by a group of six. The message written above our names was "Welcome home."

It was a homecoming to remember. The day expanded to include more relatives, and the Norwegian language was the only language spoken by our hosts. It was a great day.

When we were in Stockholm 40 years earlier, we tried every way we then thought possible to research Norene's ancestry in Norway. Her great grandfather, Hans Nøste, was a sailor who decided to try life in Australia. He took his name from his home village of Nøste in Norway, which we understood was located on Eresfjord. We also believed that the family name he had left behind was Kofoed.

I had shared a room at the Gösta Åbergh design office with a Norwegian architect, Ole, and I quizzed him regarding place names. He was unable to help with Nøste. He thought there would likely be an Eresfjord in Norway, but he had no idea where that might be. Several hours at the Stockholm library did not help.

When we left Stockholm at the beginning of the northern summer of 1964, we were set up for months of camping through Norway, Finland, the Soviet Union and central Europe. Our small tent and porta-gas cylinder were packed in the Renault's trunk with our belongings. Some of our other luggage lay across the back seat. The trip was a significant one. It culminated in my invitation to teach at the Ohio State University.

On the second afternoon of our journey, we filled the petrol tank of the Renault at a small-town garage and picked up a detailed map to see where the roads ahead might take us. Further along, we stopped at a large rock. While resting there with our new map, our eyes alighted on Eresfjord, with a small dot for Nøste on the edge of the fjord. With excitement, we jumped in the car, abandoned the plan to take the roads to the north and turned to go a little south of west—to Nøste.

It was past 10 pm when we arrived. The northern sky still lit up the quiet village, and we saw only one person. He was walking by the side of the road. I stopped the car and Norene asked in Norwegian if he knew anyone in the town with the name Kofoed.

The next thing I knew, I was running behind the car with Norene driving and the man sitting in the passenger seat. I followed the receding tail-lights along the road for several minutes and then into the front yard of a simple wooden cottage with a sod roof.

By the time I arrived, a group of men, women and children were standing at the door, showing Norene a wedding photograph of the sailor, Hans, with an envelope postmarked Sydney many years before. Norene recognised the photograph because it was the same one her father valued. This was the last communication that the Kofoed family had received from Hans, and there had been no contact between the Norwegian and Australian families since that time. The unsuccessful research in Stockholm had made it seem that it was likely to stay that way.

We stayed with the family for a few days, walked around the edge of the fjord and filled in the names of family onto the blanks of a family tree. We sat around the kitchen table and enjoyed the variety of bread and local cheese.

It was a memorable homecoming—as was our reunion in Ålesund 40 years on.

Home away from home

There were several times during our years abroad when we felt homesick for Australia. As we were driving in Mexico towards Panama, we stopped to watch the sunset from the wharves at Acapulco. Only the Pacific Ocean separated us from our home, and the presence of a cruise ship getting ready to leave accentuated the feelings of being away from family.

After weeks on the Pan American Highway, the ship's passage to Barcelona and the drive north, it was exciting to come to Edinburgh.

After meeting with my advisors at the departments of architecture and social sciences, we drove across the Firth of Forth and camped for another three weeks while waiting to move into a house in Edinburgh.

The small town of Culross and the fishing villages along the coast of Fife and Aberdeenshire had great appeal. The sight of boats and nets at places such as Crail reminded me of my early life in Australia.

One day, we returned to the small, protected harbour at Pittenween, where I thought a sequence of spaces could form the basis for a pilot study that could lead into my research. As soon as we parked the car, an elderly woman came hurrying towards us.

"I was afraid I would miss you," she said. "I saw your car with Ohio plates, and I wanted to meet you."

Even though she had been expecting Americans, Mrs Elizabeth Farfan was pleased to hear our Australian accents—or at least what remained of them. She had relatives in both Australia and America.

She invited us to her cottage at the edge of the sea. It was a white 17th-century building with hand-painted designs on the wooden ceiling of the main room.

She opened her heart and home to Norene and me.

"You're always welcome here" she told us. "This is your home away from home."

We settled into life in Scotland. Norene found work as a physiotherapist at a hospital on the road to Glasgow, and I travelled by bus to Princes Street in Edinburgh and up the hill to the university.

Edinburgh is a wonderful city and, apart from an occasional crossing of the Firth to visit Elizabeth Farfan, it provided for all our needs. Norene and I were busy.

As the writing of my thesis was nearing completion, I travelled down to London by train to be interviewed by the dean of the Faculty of Architecture at the University of Newcastle, Australia. He was visiting the United Kingdom and took the opportunity to interview applicants for a teaching position in design and architectural history.

I defended the University of Edinburgh dissertation and received word that my application to teach at the University of Newcastle was successful. The idea of going home to Australia after six years was indeed attractive.

My first home

Coming home was more than returning to Australia. It was returning to the familiar places of my early years. My first home was on Stoney Creek in Toronto, New South Wales, and it is to this region that Norene and I have returned after our various travels.

In my early years, I knew times were difficult. The Depression had left many out of work. Dad later told us how he worked as a fisherman during those years and carried a fish-basket on his arm, selling fish from door to door. Some could not afford to pay for fish; others said they couldn't. In any case, he left them a fish dinner.

Then the approach of World War II into the Pacific led authorities to require that all boats be brought to the lakeshore at the Rathmines Airforce Base. The boat-owners looked away as their boats were hitched to horses and dragged across the sand and gravel from the lake to the hillside. No foreign army would be able to use the boats.

I remember the day of excitement in 1945 when Australia celebrated the end of the war. The joy continued as the boats were brought back. After repairs, some were tied again on Stoney Creek, just across the dirt road from our house.

I loved my dad's fishing boat. Sometimes I was permitted to accompany him as he set out at dusk for a night's fishing. We travelled into the darkness, accompanied by the rhythm of a four-stroke engine. I was sure I would stay awake, but that enthusiasm was always drowned with sleep somewhere through the night. I was tucked in a blanket on the floor of the boat, and the next thing I heard was the sound of lead sinkers as the net was pulled across the roller at the stern.

Then, under a yellow ochre sky, I watched as small fish were taken from the net and thrown overboard, while the larger ones were dropped onto the floor of the boat. Occasionally, my excitement would reach a high point as a stingray, eel or saltwater catfish was lifted across the bow then returned to the lake. The edible varieties of fish included whiting, flathead, flounder, and a small version of red snapper we called squire.

Our family excursions centred on the boat. After a picnic on the lake shore, we would stop the boat for a spot of fishing. We used lines with hooks wound onto slabs of cork. The bait was threaded onto the hook and the line let down so that the sinker held the waving bait just above the sandy bottom. The line crossed over my index finger while I waited to react to a fish's bite. I was alert to the possibilities and imagined the different species approaching my bait in different ways. A flounder would suck, small squire would nibble, and a flathead would likely take the hook as well as the bait in a sudden snap.

I was six years old when Dad received a letter from the Sanitarium Health Food Company at Cooranbong in response to his request to be contacted should there be an opportunity to work at the factory. He was keen for his two boys to attend the Avondale School owned by the church, and later Avondale College.

The move from fishing and Stoney Creek was both deliberate and long-term. One move would achieve all our parents wanted. We did not own a car. That came much later. So, to get to Cooranbong, we slowly made our way in our fishing boat across Lake Macquarie to Dora Creek and then up the creek to the site of the food factory. The primary objective was to purchase a piece of land on the shore of Dora Creek and build a house. We knew that our fishing boat and a skiff would be needed to take both a factory worker and school students back and forth across the creek.

On our arrival at the factory wharf, we found a site nearby and pitched our tent, ready to begin house hunting. One night, a "southerly buster," complete with high winds and hail, demolished our tent. Avondale College kindly permitted us to move temporarily into the woodshop.

I remember one day that was very discouraging. Our parents, with us boys in tow, walked for miles in the heat and dust. Late in the afternoon, Mother felt inclined to stop at a two-storey house set back from the road. We were not in the market to buy real estate that in any way approached the size of this house, but Mother's interest was piqued by a vacant lot next door.

We waited in a spot of shade while Dad went to the house. He came back excited. At the door, a kind lady had listened to his story, and during the conversation the nearby town of Martinsville was mentioned. My mother had lived in Martinsville in her teens. When Dad mentioned her name—Pearl Hawkins—the lady told him to go and get her. We were all invited in and, before long, arrangements were made for us to share a part of the house. Our needs were met—work, school and a place to live on the shore of Dora Creek until Dad could locate a building lot and begin to construct a house.

The details for our move to Cooranbong were simple. Most of the family belongings would be carried across the dirt road at Stoney Creek to our fishing boat and skiff for the day's journey. But we also needed to hire of a small truck and driver to take a few pieces of heavy furniture by road.

I do not know how it happened, but I was given the chance to ride in the truck. It is my first memory of riding in any road vehicle. Water and rail had defined my travel horizons to that point. Being in the cab of a truck, bouncing along the gravel road to Cooranbong was an exciting new experience. I saw the wider extent of the Australian bush, the backdrop of the Watagan Mountains and the entrance to Cooranbong—the town where I would go to school.

The truck driver stopped at the small co-op store in Cooranbong to ask directions. While waiting in the cab, I saw another first. Children were riding miniature bicycles, no more than 45 centimetres (1.5 feet) high. I saw a small girl riding there that afternoon. Later, I would meet her at school. I sat behind her and was known to dip her hair in the inkwell—but only occasionally. Her name was Norene.

She has shared my passion for art and architecture, and a love for travel that has been part of our life journey together.

Homecomings

In 1963, as recent graduates from the University of Sydney, we left Australia for Europe. Six years later, we returned and built a home at Silverwater on Lake Macquarie. The view was to the fishing grounds where Dad had steered his boat at night from Stoney Creek, Toronto.

Often after a morning of meetings and lectures at the University of Newcastle, I came home, walked the short distance to Dad's house, and asked: "Do you think they're biting?"

Dad would immediately pick up the lines, bucket and bait, and I would carry the outboard motor to his boat. It was a small version of the earlier fishing boat. Sitting together, with only the occasional amplified barking of a dog from the shore, we shared quiet moments and spoke only a few words. The morning's work at the university seemed to be of another day.

In 1980, Norene and I left Australia as a family of four. Andrews University in Michigan had honoured me with the invitation to be the Inaugural Professor of Architecture. Twenty-six years later, Norene and I returned to Australia and Lake Macquarie. We became residents of the village of Wangi Wangi, 10 kilometres (6 miles) from Stoney Creek. I enjoyed the thought of being born in Toronto and retiring in Wangi.

From our home, I could see the imaginary line of a boat's wake, where in 1947 a fishing boat pulled a skiff loaded with my family's belongings towards the mouth of Dora Creek and on to Avondale.

Our last move was back to Avondale, but this time we did not need to live on the shore of Dora Creek.

There are practical and emotional aspects of homecoming. It is hardly surprising that I see a link to architecture. I enjoy thinking of the way the French architect Le Corbusier organised his workday. In the mornings, he created sculptures and paintings. In the afternoons, architectural projects. He could describe the practical—the house is a machine for living in—and the emotional. It was a deliberate balance of creative pursuit and theory, but in his definition of architecture the emotional won. He wanted buildings to touch the heart.

The philosophical focus to life is to dwell—to be at home.

To come home is about location and being united with family and friends. "To dwell" is more than a country, town and street number. Homecoming is important because it is of the mind and the heart.

The Dutch architect Aldo van Eyck summarised his thoughts on design in this way: "Architecture can do no more, and must not do less, than assist one's homecoming."

Meaningful journeys are just like that and involve a homecoming. For life, there is another Homecoming that is important because of its spiritual relevance. For us all, life journeys can do no more and should do no less than assist our Homecoming.

LIFE SYNOPSIS

1940	Neville Clouten born at Toronto, New South Wales (NSW), Australia Norene Clouten (nee Rippon) born at Cooranbong, NSW
1957	Commenced Bachelor of Architecture degree at the University of Sydney
1962	Art course with Lloyd Rees and fifth-year studio with George Molnar Married Norene Rippon Completed Bachelor of Architecture degree
1963	Worked as researcher and official guide, Sydney Opera House Left Sydney on the *Fair Sky* to travel in Europe
1963–64	Worked as an architect in Stockholm
1964–66	Studied with Professor Perry Borchers at Ohio State University Completed research projects in architectural photogrammetry
1966	Completed Master of Architecture degree at Ohio State University Drove from Ohio to Edinburgh, via Mexico, Central America and Barcelona
1969	Completed Doctor of Philosophy degree at University of Edinburgh

1969–80	Lecturer/Senior Lecturer at University of Newcastle, Australia Research in photogrammetric recording of Australian Aboriginal art
1970	Son Bjorn born
1972	Daughter Kirstin born
1974	Fellow of the Royal Australian Institute of Architects (FRAIA)
1980	Appointed Inaugural Professor of Architecture, Andrews University
1980–90	Chair, Department of Architecture, and Director of External Relations, Andrews University
1990–2004	Dean, College of Architecture and Design, Lawrence Technological University, Southfield, Michigan
2000	Received the AIA Michigan President's Award from the American Institute of Architects.
2003–13	Watercolour workshops on cruise ships
2006	Retirement in Australia
2011	Start of story with Faith Ouma, orphan girl in Rapogi, Western Kenya

THANKS

I am pleased to acknowledge the teams and individuals who have made this book a reality. Nathan Brown and Lauren Webb at Signs Publishing have supported me throughout the publication process. Thank you, Lauren, for your multitude of questions and for your thoroughness in critiquing the manuscript. Any errors or deficiencies, however, belong to me. I also thank Shane Winfield for his design work. You have continued the elegance of Thorncrown Chapel, Arkansas, in creating the book's cover.

My wife Norene gave me licence to monopolise the computer while she fitted in the tasks that keep the family afloat and on track. Thank you, my love. We share stories that come from the privilege to travel. I dedicate this book to you.

Thank you to all my friends and colleagues on several continents. Your sensitivity and willingness to share your expertise is greatly appreciated.

Dr Neville Clouten is an architect, award-winning academic, administrator and artist. He was the Inaugural Professor of Architecture at Andrews University and has also held positions at the University of Newcastle, Australia, and Lawrence Technological University, Michigan.

He is a Fellow of the Royal Australian Institute of Architects and was awarded the American Institute of Architects Michigan 2000 President's Award. He has authored more than 50 publications for architecture, science, religion and education journals.

In addition, he is an artist with watercolours in private collections and corporate offices.

Dr Neville Clouten and his wife Dr Norene, with whom he is pictured here, have been involved in humanitarian work, including helping to establish a school for orphans and disadvantaged children in Kenya.